WITTGENSTEIN
Conversations
1949–1951

WITTGENSTEIN

*Edited, with an
introduction by*

J. L. CRAFT *and*
RONALD E. HUSTWIT

Conversations
1949–1951

by O. K. BOUWSMA

HACKETT PUBLISHING COMPANY
INDIANAPOLIS

Ludwig Wittgenstein: 1889–1951

Cover design by Jackie Lacy
Interior design by J. M. Matthew

For further information, address
Hackett Publishing Company, Inc.
P. O. Box 44937
Indianapolis, Indiana 46204

Library of Congress Cataloging-in-Publication Data

Bouwsma, O. K.
Wittgenstein : conversations, 1949–1951.

Bibliography: p.
1. Wittgenstein, Ludwig, 1889–1951.
2. Bouwsma, O. K.
I. Wittgenstein, Ludwig, 1889–1951.   II. Craft, J. L.,
1947–   III. Hustwit, Ronald E., 1942–
IV. Title.
B3376.W564B684   1986   192   85-27222
ISBN 0-87220-009-4
ISBN 0-87220-008-6 (pbk.)

CONTENTS

Preface   vii

Introduction   ix

Chronology of Wittgenstein's life   xxxiii

Conversations   1

     Cornell, July 1949   3

     Smith College, October 1949   45

     Oxford, August 1950–January 1951   53

Further reading   77

PREFACE

Wittgenstein Conversations, 1949–1951 consists of a set of notes which O. K. Bouwsma wrote after numerous discussions with Ludwig Wittgenstein during that time. It is a part of the collection of Bouwsma's papers now housed in the Humanities Research Center at the University of Texas at Austin. Bouwsma's original entries were written in the daily notebook form which he had long practiced. Those notes pertaining to Wittgenstein were subsequently separated from the other notebooks and assembled and typed. Bouwsma occasionally showed these notes, or portions of them, to friends but did not want them circulated. This book makes the notes on Wittgenstein available to the public for the first time. We have edited them, made some minor deletions, and prepared an introduction which aims at providing the historical setting together with some general philosophical orientation.

We must thank Professor Kenneth Johnson, Morris Lazerowitz, Alice Ambrose Lazerowitz, and Mrs. Gertrude Bouwsma-Bos for their help in preparing the introduction to the *Conversations*. Thanks also to Barbara Hustwit for typing the manuscript. We also acknowledge support from the Bouwsma family, the University of Texas at Austin Humanities Research Center, and the College of Wooster. The latter, through several grants from the Faculty Development Fund, made travel and manuscript reproductions possible.

INTRODUCTION

OETS KOLK BOUWSMA was born of Dutch-American parents in Muskegon, Michigan, 1898. He was educated at Calvin College and at the University of Michigan where he was a student of English literature and philosophy. In his early years he was an advocate of idealism, most notably Hegel's philosophy, but later found the work of G. E. Moore, the refutations of idealism, more compatible. He worked intensely on Moore, publishing papers on him and sending his students from the University of Nebraska, where he taught for nearly forty years, to study with him at Cambridge. Bouwsma's reputation as a young philosopher was associated with his work on Moore. The Schilpp volume on G. E. Moore (The Library of Living Philosophers series) contains one of Bouwsma's papers critical of Moore's work and shows Moore's respect for Bouwsma in his reply. Bouwsma's reputation on Moore resulted in his being invited to deliver the John Locke Lectures at Oxford and in his being President of the American Philosophical Association. Later his reputation developed in connection with Wittgenstein.

One of several students whom he encouraged to go to England to work with G. E. Moore was Norman Malcolm. Through working with Moore, Malcolm came into contact with Wittgenstein, attending lectures and having discussions that shaped his philosophical development. After the war, Malcolm returned to teach philosophy at Cornell, and it was from there in 1949 that he was able to persuade Wittgenstein to visit and have discussions with Cornell faculty and students. Malcolm was also able to arrange for Bouwsma to teach at Cornell during Wittgenstein's visit. By then Bouwsma had become a serious student of Wittgenstein's dictations, which were later published as *The Blue Book*.

After the personal influence of Wittgenstein and much hard work on the *Philosophical Investigations*, Bouwsma began to emerge as one who could apply Wittgenstein's methods to a variety of philosophical problems, such as the skeptical thought of Descartes and Berkeley or to such perennial puzzles as time, truth, and thinking. He taught at the University of Nebraska until 1965, having his greatest influence through the many graduate students he trained in his unique style of discussion and in listening for the sense of a philosophical sentence. Although he wrote incessantly and presented numerous papers, he published only one book—a collection of essays titled *Philosophical Essays*. After retirement at Nebraska, he accepted an invitation from the University of Texas to continue his teaching. He did so in the same manner and with the same results until his death in 1978. He was, at that time, as active and productive in writing and teaching as ever. His papers and daily notebooks, the latter filling hundreds of legal pads, were deposited after his death in the Humanities Research Center in Austin, Texas. Two collections of his papers have since been published as books: *Toward a New Sensibility* and *Without Proof or Evidence.*

In July 1949, at Norman Malcolm's invitation and with his encouragement, Ludwig Wittgenstein came to Cornell University and stayed with the Malcolms. According to an account of that visit in Malcolm's memoir, the following philosophers were on campus during his stay: John Nelson, Willis Doney, Max Black, Stuart Brown, and a number of Cornell graduate students. Bouwsma was there as well, having come from Lincoln, Nebraska, at Malcolm's invitation.

Malcolm reports that Wittgenstein had various talks with these individuals, some separately and some in groups, over the summer and into the fall. Of Bouwsma he relates: "With Oets Bouwsma and me he began to read Frege's paper, 'Über Sinn und Bedeutung' (On Sense and Reference); and this led to two or three meetings in which Wittgenstein expounded his divergence from Frege. Then in one meeting we discussed free will and determinism" (Malcolm's *Ludwig Wittgenstein: A Memoir*, 2d ed., p. 70). Accounts of these discussions appear in Bouwsma's notes along with references to the above-mentioned Cornell philosophers. There is also a wide range of topics discussed beyond those included in Bouwsma's notes. There were other discussions with Malcolm in which Bouwsma did not participate, discussions about Moore's work which later take form in Wittgenstein's *On Certainty*, and, presumably, still other discussions of which no record exists.

The reader of Bouwsma's notes will quickly see that there was a special relationship between Bouwsma and Wittgenstein from the very beginning that was grounded in mutual recognition of personal depth and philosophical seriousness. To be sure, Wittgenstein was the teacher and Bouwsma the learner, but what a remarkable learner Bouwsma was for Wittgenstein to open up to him so, and how interesting their meetings must have been to influence Bouwsma so pervasively.

During the summer at Cornell, Bouwsma's meetings with Wittgenstein took several different forms. Sometimes they were in small groups in someone's home; sometimes Bouwsma, Malcolm, and Wittgenstein met in Malcolm's garden or basement. Often Wittgenstein and Bouwsma would take walks together or Bouwsma would take Wittgenstein by car to the Finger-lake countryside. On these walks, as in their later discussions, Bouwsma generally proposed some topic for discussion and Wittgenstein would quickly take off with it. Their relationship was not dialectical; Bouwsma does not oppose or present counter-examples. Rather he is searching Wittgenstein's remarks for their meaning and working to understand them, as he writes them down. They are understanding each other as they talk, Bouwsma with more difficulty, trying to grasp Wittgenstein's insights and pictures.

This practice of taking walks for the occasion to discuss philosophy continued throughout their friendship. In a letter, Morris Lazerowitz reports the same practice when Wittgenstein came to visit Bouwsma in mid-October at Smith College in Northampton, Massachusetts. "Wittgenstein came to Northampton and stayed with the Bouwsmas for two or three days," Lazerowitz explains, "during which Oets and Wittgenstein took walks and had some discussions, with Wittgenstein taking the lion's share of the talk." References to such walks appear repeatedly throughout the notes and provide the most frequent setting for their discussions.

Bouwsma went on to Smith College where he was a sabbatical-leave replacement for the fall term. This appointment was secured through his friends Morris Lazerowitz and Alice Ambrose Lazerowitz. Bouwsma arrived there from Cornell with his wife, Gertrude, and his daughter, Gretchen, the youngest of their three children. They are mentioned several times in the notes; and on more than one occasion, Wittgenstein's discussions with Gretchen about her school work led to discussions with Bouwsma about literature and education. A dated entry in the notes for October 11, 1949, indicates that the two men had resumed their walks and discussions. Wittgenstein stayed for three days, and then after a short time returned to England in late October. This was the last Bouwsma would see of him until the following summer.

Because of his reputation for his work on Moore, Bouwsma was asked to deliver the John Locke Lectures at Oxford in 1950–51. The invitation was a mark of distinction and Bouwsma was the first American asked to present them. During part of that year, Wittgenstein also lived in Oxford. He made a five-week trip to Norway and some other trips to Cambridge where his physician, Dr. Edward Bevan, practiced. (By now Wittgenstein had been diagnosed as having cancer.) But primarily he stayed in Oxford where his presence provided the opportunity for him and Bouwsma to renew their friendship and their practice of discussing philosophy. The notes begin again then, after about a nine-month interval, with the date August 17, 1950, and continue until Wittgenstein's death in April 1951. However, the reader will notice that there are more discussions recorded than there are dated entries.

Though Wittgenstein was seriously ill during this period, his health fluctuated. At times he was able to work and hold vigorous discussions; at others, he experienced dark periods and despaired of ever being able to work again. Mrs. Bouwsma frequently prepared broth and applesauce for him; he remarked in a letter to Malcolm: "I am just good enough to eat applesauce with a philosopher." Despite his low periods and inability to work, the notes reveal the presence of a clear and powerful mind.

During the time at Oxford Bouwsma and Wittgenstein continued their practice of taking walks together to discuss philosophy. Sometimes they would sit on benches outdoors, sometimes Wittgenstein would come to the Bouwsma's house for a meal or to roust him out for a walk. But the walking discussion seemed to be the norm: "Today we walked...today we walked out through the meadow...today we walked along the canal." This is philosophizing in the peripatetic tradition. There is no record of others being involved in these discussions. Anscombe was in Oxford, and Wittgenstein had introduced Bouwsma to his friend-student Yorick Smythies. But while Bouwsma refers to some ideas of Anscombe and Smythies, there is nothing in the notes about any combined discussions involving these or other philosophers. The recorded discussions are between Bouwsma and Wittgenstein and concern topics that Bouwsma introduces or topics arising spontaneously out of something that they saw or mentioned on their walks. This was Bouwsma's opportunity to have access to one of the great minds of our age. He did not waste it.

When Bouwsma returned to Nebraska in 1951 after his two-year sojourn, he wrote to his friend and former student Kenneth Johnson that in Wittgenstein he "saw what struck me as the height of perspecuity, the most intense intellectual activity, the swiftest and keenest mind I have met. It was like a miracle. His words were like a beam of light through a fog in almost any conversation." Several weeks later, on December 1, 1951, he wrote the following in a note for a class on the nature of a prophet:

> What is a prophet like? Wittgenstein is the nearest
> to a prophet I have ever known. He is a man who is like a
> tower, who stands high and unattached, leaning on no
> one. He has his own feet. He fears no man. "Nothing can
> hurt me!" But other men fear him. And why? Not at all
> because he can strike them or take their money or their
> good names. They fear his judgement. And so I feared
> Wittgenstein, felt responsible to him. I always knew how
> precious a walk and talk with him was, and yet I was in
> dread of his coming and of being with him. I was in fear
> too that I should have to give an account to him of my
> John Locke Lectures, why I consented to give them—
> since he had refused, and what should I say. I breathed
> easier when he went to Norway, and later when he went
> to Cambridge. He was my judge in respect to anything I

might say, and I felt responsible to him. I could not shrug him off or say: What do I care? When he went away, I felt free.

I do not think that I have ever felt this way about anyone else. Of course, I feared him, but at the same time I realized that my hopes in my work were all vested in him. His words I cherished like jewels. And do so now. But the main point is that he robbed me of a lazy comfort in my own mediocrity. There is no one to whom I owed so much, no one to whom I listened as I listened to him, no one whom I have feared, no one who was so clearly my rightful judge, my superior. In the presence or in the hearing of other men I recognized nothing of this sort. Here I judge. But in this case of Wittgenstein it is almost, it has come as, a relief to see that he made mistakes.

In any case the acquaintance with Wittgenstein has given me some inkling as to what the power of the prophet was among his people. "Thus saith the Lord" is the token of that being high above all fear and all blandishment, fearless and feared, judge and conscience. Thus saith the Lord!

It is an awful thing to work under the gaze and questioning of such piercing eyes, and such discernment, knowing rubbish and gold! And one who speaks the word: "This is rubbish!"

Beginning in this year, Bouwsma's notepads begin to take the form familiar to many of his students and colleagues. The form consists of lengthy, patient notes in which he attempts to work out Wittgenstein's ideas and techniques for himself. They are, most frequently, preparations for and responses to students in seminars, readings of Wittgenstein's *Philosophical Investigations* or other works in philosophy, or accounts of discussions with friends and colleagues. The *Philosophical Investigations* was published in spring 1953 and provided the meat for Bouwsma's diet from then until his death in 1978. He returns to the themes of the *Philosophical Investigations* over and over again, expressing them in his own words with new examples and applications. It is well nigh impossible to count the times in the notepads that he takes up some form of the question: What is the meaning of a word? or the times he considers the mistaken idea that the meaning of a word is the object for which it stands.

For Bouwsma, the discipline of writing and working through ideas for himself was always there, but the new direction and new ways of working in philosophy as the result of Wittgenstein's influence appear most dramatically here in 1951. Ten years later, Bouwsma, again writing to Kenneth Johnson, remarks: "One thing I know is that one does not understand Wittgenstein until he is able, not to repeat what he says, but to work with his ideas. The latter requires long practice." It was in his notepads that Bouwsma acquired his understanding of Wittgenstein.

Bouwsma's work habits, evident in the notepads, indicate the great change he underwent following his meetings with Wittgenstein:

> It was in the summer of '39 I first came upon certain student notes of Wittgenstein during a visit with the Lazerowitzs in New England. The *Tractatus* which you have no doubt heard of was much earlier and had never made much of an impression upon me. I had heard of Wittgenstein, of course, but especially through these two former students of mine of whom I'm sure I had

spoken to you—Malcolm and Lazerowitz. Well, those
notes, boot-legged, and circulated too, against Wittgenstein's wishes, I studied, and they made a powerful impression on me. I was ready for the revolutionary conceptions
which I met in them. Working as I had with my own
meager resources and with Moore I had come to a stop. I
was also fallow, and Wittgenstein fell upon me like seed.
For ten years I spaded and dug and watered as I was able,
working out hints I had picked up in those notes.

While those bootlegged notes played an important role in
this change, it was the actual meetings with Wittgenstein that had the greatest effect on Bouwsma. In
such personal encounters he learned to "fear his judgement," to "cherish his words," and realized that he,
Bouwsma, was being "robbed of a lazy comfort." These
are strong words to use in connection with a relationship
of one human being to another.

The reader of these notes may well ask: What was
there about Wittgenstein, as reflected in these conversations, that made him so impressive to Bouwsma? The
Conversations contain relatively little discussion of the
basic themes of the *Philosophical Investigations*. Only
once or twice is there discussion of the meaning of a
word being its use, and then there is no full treatment of
that idea. Neither does the reader get any sense that
Wittgenstein was presenting his philosophy to Bouwsma
or trying to teach Bouwsma what he was about. So it was
not a new philosophy or doctrine that Bouwsma stood in
awe of. It was something else. What was it?

The *Conversations* begin with a description of
Wittgenstein—Bouwsma's first impressions. Bouwsma
drives to the train station to pick up Malcolm and Witt-

genstein, who are arriving from New York. He reports
that Wittgenstein has an easy and friendly manner.
Bouwsma seems relieved to discover this, since there had
been abundant reports that Wittgenstein could be difficult. At the first discussion, Bouwsma finds that there is
an "intensity and impatience about him which are
enough, certainly, to frighten one." He goes on to remark
that he doubts if Wittgenstein could bear idle talk and
unintelligibility gladly. Bouwsma then steels himself for
Wittgenstein's scrutiny because he believes that there is
much to learn and gain by subjecting himself to Wittgenstein's harsh judgements. It is the intensity of Wittgenstein and his severe judgements that come through
immediately in these first impressions and throughout
the *Conversations*. Wittgenstein's mind is always working, and working hard—even in small matters. To
Bouwsma's remark that Wittgenstein is a good walker,
he replies that he is not a good walker at all. But it is not
as if he is deliberately trying to be difficult; he is, rather,
simply taking Bouwsma's small talk seriously. When the
Bouwsmas are invited to the Malcolms' home for tea,
Malcolm, Bouwsma, and Wittgenstein are separated
from the non-philosophers in the house because Wittgenstein could not tolerate social chit-chat. And when
they discuss philosophy where the mental energy
required is so much greater, Wittgenstein's intensity is
impressive.

    The intensity in the philosophy takes many
forms. The reader can see it in the quickness with which
Wittgenstein replies to Bouwsma's suggested topics and
in the way that first response so often penetrates to the
heart of the matter. When Bouwsma proposes, for exam-

ple, that they discuss hedonism, particularly the idea that we do everything for pleasure, Wittgenstein remarks immediately, "Obviously this is no empirical remark." He goes on to develop that idea. But this is a kind of gem that has great philosophic value. It shows in a flash that the central sentence of hedonism is a generalization through which all human action is viewed, allowing no counterexample. It reminds us of how easily misled we are by general statements and invites us to recall to mind how the words *want* and *pleasure* are used and related to each other. There is more, but all this is a working out of the first remark quickly given in response to an idea.

Wittgenstein's intensity and impatience are revealed in his judgements of others. Some of the more personal judgements, particularly of those still alive, have been removed from the text by the editors, but those of other philosophers and ideas remain and show the severity that made people fear him. Of Socrates' interlocutors, he says they are ninnies who never have any arguments of their own; of Whitehead and Russell, that they were good once but had continued to write after they had stopped thinking; and of attending lectures on Shakespeare and translating lyric poetry, that these were bad and unthinkable, respectively. With respect to what Bouwsma did in class, it may well have been "futile," "trifling," or "too risky."

But the discussions do not reveal a man speaking this way out of vanity. It is not Wittgenstein's aim to reduce the size of others so that he might loom large. He is severe with himself as well. He complains of his own stupidity and apologizes for failing to produce helpful examples. Malcolm reports that Wittgenstein had the same worry about himself that he had of Russell and Whitehead—that he would stop thinking and die mentally. This is not the same as worrying that he would become senile. This is the worry that he would lose his intensity, his passion for thinking hard enough to give a philosophical problem the attention it required and deserved. His judgements were not those of a petty mind, but those reflecting a sharp and energetic intelligence. And this was not only impressive to Bouwsma, who, in the eyes of those who knew him, also knew how to judge; but it was also, for Bouwsma, a test of his own willingness to learn. In subjecting himself to Wittgenstein's judgements, he was recognizing their power and clarity and showing his own desire to work in philosophy with that sort of clarity and attention.

The traits of intensity, disdain for small talk, and capacity to judge in Wittgenstein are, of course, interrelated and inseparable from each other and from other traits and aspects of his character. This intensity shows in his quick responses and in his critical aptness and also in his insightful analogies and pictures. Here are samples of the latter:

> There is a picture here ... Imagine I'm an invisible engineer ...

> Now it's as though everything on the map represents something but representing is not represented on the map.

> Imagine a lamp on a post. And a light in the lamp ... steady succession of light is passing through the lamp-frame. This is James's stream of consciousness.

> We may compare language to money ...

> Imagine a tribe who when they viewed things horrible, loathsome to us, clapped their hands ...

And so on. These are marvelous pictures which illuminate the darkness of philosophical thoughts and puzzles.

The picture often aims at showing how someone is looking at a particular subject. In connection with their discussion of Descartes' *cogito*, for example, the image is that of a movie projector. The past is on the roll behind and the future is on the roll ahead, but where is the present? It is only the frame which is before the light. This picture illustrates how Descartes was thinking of the self and what could be known of it. It is not that Descartes thought in these terms: rather, the metaphor is a way of visualizing Descartes' *cogito* and illustrating its grammatical confusion. It also presents some of the essential puzzlement of the *cogito*. One can now see the difficulty in talking about the self—the I—which only exists in a single present frame before the light.

Wittgenstein's picture enables one to see how Descartes' sentences were generated and what their source of meaning appeared to be. It also suggests new lines of questions, confusions, and observations. One should not overlook this simple fact, either: the ability to visualize such abstract ideas in such vivid ways is impressive to a learner. The right analogy or image in the mind of one who is working to understand is like a light going on in the dark or like relief from distress. It is an impression which lasts. One who has worked hard to get such a clear view of a philosophical problem is sufficiently impressed by the one who is able to produce such pictures. And with Wittgenstein they were abundant.

There is in these pictures an element of surprise, an unexpected turn which orients one's way of thinking. They make things suddenly clear or open up another's thought in an astonishing way. One has the impression that the producer of the picture is someone special. This sense that Wittgenstein was special and different comes through in many of his responses to Bouwsma's remarks and to things he notices in their surroundings. The associations, the formed opinions, the questions, the observations all bespeak a uniquely well-read, self-disciplined thinker—one who commanded attention and captured interest.

On a walk the two philosophers see a sign for cheeseburgers. Wittgenstein begins telling Bouwsma of a letter of Fénelon to the French Academy recommending that new words be admitted into the language only if they are "sweet." Then he discusses what "sweet" would mean. Bouwsma remarks in astonishment: "This is a fine illustration of the richness of his mind. For all this came about through what? Through seeing a sign advertising cheeseburgers. That offended him! He loathed it. That was no way to derive words. And what happens? Fénelon." Bouwsma finds this connection surprising, and a commonplace word such as *cheeseburger* is seen in a new light. Many other responses have a similar impressiveness.

While the two men are having a dish of ice cream, Wittgenstein reflects on how different this world is from the world of his parents—how the machines would have made our lives unrecognizable to them. He describes having heard John Dewey give a lecture on the kind of human being education should produce, and remarks: "But I was a human being which was fitted into the old environment." This remark captures something important about Wittgenstein's difference. He has, in a certain sense, a conservative mind. He is not at all impressed by the technological advances and scientific outlook of the twentieth century. He disdains the idea of moral progress in history and the notion that the world is a better place to live than it ever used to be. He is skeptical of the future of mankind. He attends to the detail of specific human beings' lives and does not meddle in mankind or in popular movements. He is attracted to Kierkegaard and Dostoyevsky, both of whom share and develop these thoughts. Bouwsma, too, shared them, and that helps account for their mutual attraction.

The list of unique and surprising responses goes on and on. He sees a jukebox and asks: "What is *juke?*" The Gospel of John he does not understand, but this does not mean that others do not nor that the language is vague. How do those who do understand it use their sentences? And what is clear over against it? In *Crime and Punishment* it is "most magnificent" that Raskolnikov should forget to lock the door during the murder. Modern Judaism has nothing left since sacrifice is no longer practiced. Cardinal Newman had a queer mind, not because he became a Roman Catholic (Wittgenstein's best students were converts), but because of the way he gave reasons for his conversion. In moral philosophy it is said "I ought implies I can," but this is not so in the Christian orthodox position: "Be ye perfect." One can't be perfect, but one can be commanded to try. These are remarks and responses of one who is intellectually curious and honest and who does not absorb his opinions from newspapers and general culture. If they do not stimulate one to do the same, at least they should have the effect of alerting one to the presence of a rich thinker and of making one self-conscious of one's own intellectual laxity.

One will notice that these last responses concern themes in religion and ethics. This is not a skewed sampling. Many of the discussions had to do with these topics, and Bouwsma was not always the one who introduced them. They reveal another side to Wittgenstein, the side glimpsed in the notebooks of 1914–16 and in other conversations reported by Drury and Malcolm. If one had read only the *Philosophical Investigations* or the *Tractatus*, one might well not expect this interest and sensitivity to religion in Wittgenstein. These are not what one might regard as typical conversations of an "analytic philosopher." Russell expressed astonishment in one of his letters at Wittgenstein's admiration for Kierkegaard and Dostoyevsky and at his mysticism. He writes to Lady Ottoline Morrell: "I had felt in his book a flavour of mysticism, but was astonished when I found that he has become a complete mystic. He reads people like Kierkegaard and Angelus Silesius, and he seriously contemplates becoming a monk" (*Letters to Russell, Keynes, and Moore*, p. 82). Perhaps Russell, having known Wittgenstein personally, should have expected as much, but to many readers, this aspect of Wittgenstein comes as a surprise. Whether Bouwsma was surprised or not, one cannot tell, but that he appreciated and took great interest in these remarks of Wittgenstein there can be no doubt.

Wittgenstein's work in the *Philosophical Investi-*

gations does not present a philosophical system or theory from which one can derive consistent answers to all questions and explain all phenomena. There is rather a reflection of constant struggle and appreciation for the capacity of language to confuse and mislead. Wittgenstein both practiced and taught constant vigilance in this regard, as these conversations show. In considering what made Wittgenstein appear so different and so impressive to Bouwsma, one must think of their discussions in this light. Wittgenstein was not teaching Bouwsma his theory of language nor his "philosophy." It is not as if Bouwsma were trying to get the theory down or to understand the principles of linguistic philosophy, trying one aspect and then another, seeing if Wittgenstein would correct him or affirm that he had it straight. Wittgenstein struggled on the spot with every topic that was introduced or idea that came up. He may have started off on an idea quickly, and his responses often reflected considerable previous thought about an idea, but he was working as he talked. Again, his thinking up pictures, his surprising turns of thought, and his persistence in returning to the problem, all exhibit his struggling with ideas rather than working out pat answers consistent with some supposed theory of language.

Bouwsma frequently takes note of Wittgenstein's persistence. Recalling a discussion, for example, where Bouwsma proposed that they discuss someone's lecturing on religious truth, Bouwsma writes:

> Religious truth? He went on puzzling, thinking his way. Of course it isn't botany, it isn't anything about eclipses, it isn't economics or history. ... But what is one

to say besides that? The man in Christ Church will very
likely talk about Christian dogmas. And one might make
some sense in this way, each believer talking about what
he believes. But there is no sense talking about religious
truth in general ...

Now one might say that Wittgenstein already knew
which way he wanted to go with this question, but
Bouwsma saw the puzzlement and struggle, and the
reader can see them in this account. On the one hand,
religious truth is not just any truth at all; on the other
hand, how could there be just one and only one sort of
thing that counted as religious?

Wittgenstein's continual struggle with puzzlement, his finding his way as he went along, did not have
the effect of teaching Bouwsma certain ideas. Rather, it
served as an inspiration to him—as a model of something
that he already admired and for which he already had the
right philosophical disposition. Bouwsma was not looking for a philosophy of life; he already had the equivalent
of that in Christianity. Neither was he looking for a
theory of language. He was looking for a way of working
in philosophy that reflected his lost faith in metaphysics,
his desire for clarity, and his desire not to be taken in.
Some of this longing is captured in his 1941 notebook
remark about Moore: "Like Moses, Moore took us to the
promised land, had a glimpse of it, but never enjoyed it
himself." Moore provided no relief, no nourishment, no
direction for Bouwsma. They were two wanderers. How
impressive Wittgenstein must have appeared then! "A
method has been found," Bouwsma noted; this was an
expression of hope for that relief, nourishment, and
direction. His essays on Moore show his admiration for

clarity and sense. He came to prefer working with details and on particular sentences rather than on the generalities of systems.

In his 1940 notebook Bouwsma writes: "I used to study books, now I study sentences." In Wittgenstein's company he must surely have been inspired by one who not only shared some of these affinities but had come to understand something of the myriad ways in which philosophy had gone wrong. Again, these notes do not show Wittgenstein teaching this to Bouwsma. But one can see, as Bouwsma did, the older man's habits of thought as a great inspiration: his clarity, his attention to detail and examples, his passion for doing philosophy, his unwillingness to take the easy way through a problem or to accept some conventional view of it, his capacity for judgement, his quickness and his honesty. These inspired similar habits of thought to grow in Bouwsma.

To be sure, the soil in Bouwsma was fertile, and the roots for many of these habits were already there. Bouwsma's ten years of working out hints on his own from *The Blue Book* and his subsequent diligent work with the *Philosophical Investigations* in the years immediately following his discussions with Wittgenstein were an inseparable part of that change and growth in habit. But the encounter with Wittgenstein itself marks the turning point for that change. The reader of the *Conversations* will find therefore not only an account of Wittgenstein's impressive presence but also the account of an essential part of Bouwsma's philosophical development. The *Conversations* are by no means complete descriptions of either, but they are an invaluable source if one has an interest in these two individuals.

It is our hope that these remarks will help prepare the reader for reading the *Conversations*—by having described the setting in which they occurred, and by having discussed how Wittgenstein went about responding to Bouwsma. A few comments concerning the text may also be helpful. Bouwsma had these notes typed and titled "Wittgenstein Notes," but in spite of all the interest others showed in them, he never published them. Occasionally he gave them to a friend who might profit from reading them. When he did show them to someone, he seems always to have made it clear that he did not want them circulated or published. Nevertheless, copies were made and the notes were circulated much more widely than Bouwsma ever realized. His reasons for not wanting them published were not entirely clear; nor was it clear that he would object to their being published at any future time. Surely some, but not all, of his reluctance had to do with the fact that some of Wittgenstein's remarks about friends and acquaintances were harsh. Certain of these individuals have reputations as professional philosophers, and some are still alive. Because of this and because the remarks would very likely be misunderstood if taken out of context, we have removed them from the text. Deleting such remarks does not gloss them over entirely. The reader, encountering the severity of Wittgenstein's judgement on Russell, for example, is likely to fill in the deleted remarks for himself.

Bouwsma may also have been reluctant to give these notes wider circulation because they were not written for publication. They were set down primarily for his own use. He wanted to keep a record of what was said and what happened. But they are not simply a diary or a travelogue. They are Bouwsma's attempts to understand what Wittgenstein was saying and to think through the discourse for himself. The reader will observe that Bouwsma does not argue with or criticize Wittgenstein's ideas. Rather, he attempts to recount long discussions several hours or days later. This involves not only his ability to remember what Wittgenstein said but also his ability to reconstruct the flow of thought in his own mind. Bouwsma, as indicated above, was of a similar disposition of mind on many of these subjects. With Wittgenstein's stimulation he goes on to recall and even finish the thoughts for himself. After receiving the *Conversations* from Bouwsma, Yorick Smythies wrote back that it was remarkable how much in tune Bouwsma and Wittgenstein were with each other. He noted that the absence of quotation marks around Wittgenstein's remarks reflected the emergence of a Bouwsma-Wittgenstein personality. The reader sometimes cannot tell who is talking. Occasionally, when clarity absolutely required it, we have added quotation marks. But we have preserved that feature of the recorded discussions which so struck Smythies.

The reader should also be aware that the dated entries do not necessarily correspond to a single discussion. Bouwsma, in writing up the conversations afterward, seems in some entries to have written up more than one discussion or more than one day's events. The last entry is dated January 16 [1951] and speaks of events and remarks that seem much closer to the time of Wittgenstein's death in April. One entry, August 17, 1950, was located in the typescript between October 1, 1950, and November 28, 1950. We have no explanation and simply inserted it in the proper sequential order.

Throughout the typescript, Bouwsma frequently uses the initials of people who were present or referred to—M. for Norman Malcolm, K. for Kierkegaard, and so on. We have supplied the complete names to help the reader who may occasionally not recognize the abbreviations. We have left W., which always stands for Wittgenstein.

In addition to these deletions and changes in the typescript, we have silently corrected a few minor errors in punctuation, spelling, and grammar. We have also made a few guesses about the spelling of proper names and on one or two words that were illegible in the typescript.

Among the people to whom Bouwsma showed the "Conversations" was Wittgenstein's nephew, Thomas Stonborough, whom Bouwsma had met on a visit to Vienna. Stonborough greatly appreciated and approved of the manuscript and upon receiving it in 1965 wrote:

> This morning your package arrived with your notes on Uncle Ludwig's visit to you. I read them at one sitting this afternoon and found them very good indeed. In fact the best thing written on him I know of. The reason for this is that you have asked yourself personal questions about him occasionally and set about answering them. According to my memory and experience, you have answered them correctly, insofar as one can ever catch the soul's motives in words. Both in the instance of his dislike for the later Russell and Whitehead as well as his outlook on teaching philosophy. A very good description of his rapidity in answering questions and the breadth of the analogies and pictures at his disposal.

Stonborough's ideas of what stands out in the

notes square nicely with our views. The letter acknowl-
edges that Bouwsma had captured something of Wittgenstein as he really was and presented him in the
positive way that he deserved. Stonborough went on to
ask if Bouwsma had an opinion about why Wittgenstein
was so kind to him. Without answering the question,
Stonborough said that he thought he knew why but
wanted to see if Bouwsma had come to the same
conclusion. We have no record of either one's answer to
that question, but anyone who spent time around
Bouwsma could supply an answer. In Bouwsma, Wittgenstein saw a deep, unpretentious, and serious
philosopher.

J. L. CRAFT
RONALD E. HUSTWIT

Chronology
of Wittgenstein's Life

1889	Born April 26 at Vienna, Austria.
1911–1913	After training originally as an engineer, attended Trinity College, Cambridge, to study philosophy with Bertrand Russell. Began work leading to the *Tractatus Logico-Philosophicus*.
1914–1918	Served in Austrian army, taken prisoner in 1918 and held near Monte Cassino, Italy. Completed *Tractatus* in August 1918.
1919–1920	Trained at a college for elementary school teachers in Vienna.
1920–1926	Taught in remote villages in the districts of Schneeberg and Semmering in Lower Austria. *Tractatus* published (1922).
1926–1928	Designed and built a mansion in Vienna for his sister, Gretl.

1929   Returned to Cambridge, submitted the *Tractatus* as a thesis, and received his Ph.D.

1930-1935   Became a Fellow of Trinity College. Lectured and wrote extensively on philosophical problems. Dictated *The Blue Book* 1933-1934, *The Brown Book* 1934-1935.

1936   Lived for over a year in Norway; began to write the *Philosophical Investigations*.

1938-1939   Returned to Cambridge. Succeeded G. E. Moore in the chair in philosophy (1939).

1940-1944   Served as a porter at Guy's Hospital in London; later worked in a medical laboratory in Newcastle.

1945-1947   Lectured and taught at Cambridge.

1949   Visited Norman Malcolm in America; met and befriended Bouwsma.

1949-1950   Returned to England; lived in Oxford. Bouwsma and his family stayed in Oxford.

1951   Died April 29 in Cambridge at the home of Dr. Bevan.

1953   *Philosophical Investigations* published.

CONVERSATIONS

*In the middle of the journey of our life,
I came to myself in the dark wood
where the straight way was lost.*

DANTE

NORMAN MALCOLM

Wittgenstein at Cornell

Cornell

July 1949

ON TUESDAY OF THIS WEEK we drove to Syracuse to meet
Norman Malcolm and Wittgenstein who had just arrived
from Europe. After all the stories about him he struck
me as a very attractive man with an easy and a friendly
manner.

And last evening, Thursday, he came with
Norman and Max Black and Stuart Brown for discussion.
And I heard and saw him perform. He uses his hands
and his head a great deal, and walks about, too. But
what characterizes his talk is the ready availability of
example and imaginary situation to clarify the uses of
expressions. There is an intensity and an impatience
about him which are enough, certainly, to frighten one,
and there was once when Norman was floundering,
going on talking, perhaps, in order to get W. to go on,
when he was nearly violent. No wonder so many people
have found him difficult. At any rate, I can imagine that
he cannot bear idle talk and unintelligibility gladly, and
he shows it. So, too, many of us must be uncomfortable.

The subject was ethics. Brown introduced the
subject, the idea that duties and rights are correlative. It
seemed to Brown that a man might very well have a duty
when no other man could claim a right to the performance of that duty. W. seized upon the use of "It
seems ..." Why "It seems ..."? Of course, a man may ...
Why not? A child may be brought up: "Never, never,
steal," "Resist tyranny," etc. He does not then owe that
duty to his parents. He must simply do or not do. A man
may owe his duty on the other hand to God, or as we see
to nothing at all. How then do people come to say that all
duties are owed to someone? Perhaps simply out of a
habit of speech in this context. Some duties are owed to
someone. Perhaps most are. This now establishes the
pattern of the language, and the expectations in connection with it. So duties are owed, and to someone.
    (It occurs to me now that this also reflects the
contract theory of morals.)
    This issue was fairly easily disposed of. Then,
Norman took up the use of "absolute" and "universal."
What would you do with: Everyone ought to be honest?
There was some confusion here. Black suggested something like this, that this injunction was the pre-supposi-
tion of all morality. The word "dogmatic" was used here
and so was "categorical." Black and Brown didn't exactly
like this. They were wanting to say that something could
be said, one could argue for this statement. But this also
was confused. You certainly could not prove any such
statements. Here talk was begun by W. about the two
tribes, he being reformer to one and Malcolm being
reformer to the other. Each now would have a different
morality, and each might be immoral to the other. There
might now be said to be different moral principles, but

one can see in the way in which they come to be held
that argument and proof have nothing to do with it. I
introduced the illustration, "Pride is an evil," with
which I worked in my ethics class, and said that when I
did this, all that happened was that the idea was clarified,
and sometimes I won some students. The point was that
one can exhibit the sort of thing one has in mind, and
that is all.

Later in the living room—our conversation earlier
was in the garden—the subject was resumed. How did I
exhibit "pride"? By reading from *The Brothers
Karamazov.* W. seemed to approve of this but he made
some objection which I did not understand. He said
somebody else might write a different book, apparently
exhibiting pride in a different light. The point seemed to
be that what is relevant is patterns of life which are
enmeshed with all sorts of other things, and so this
makes the matter much more complex than at first it
seemed. Perhaps this is it. Pride is, in anyone's life,
always only a part. No man is pride alone. Pride is speci-
fied in a context of other interests and of other human
beings. It is this total situation in which pride infects
with evil. Pride is like an infection, a fever. It isn't
located like a sore thumb. The fever permeates the
whole body. So pride too. This is nice. I was glad to be
reminded of this.

From this point we went on from a suggestion of
Norman's: Suppose Cesare Borgia said, "This is my ethical principle: I trample on other men's toes all I can."
Norman was fascinated by his having stuck pins
(Cleopatra) into people. At that W. frowned. Ethical
principle! Not everything is an ethical principle. How is
an ethical principle identified? This took us into the use

of the expression "ethical." Nothing precise of course. A
principle is ethical by virtue of its surroundings. What
surroundings? You could imagine "surroundings" where
one was justified and enjoined upon to enjoy sufferings,
the sufferings of the wicked, for instance. At any rate
there are limits surely to what is an "ethical" principle.
It reminds me now of Herbert Feigl's "choosing
principles."

July 31

THIS AFTERNOON we went to Norman and Lee's, I thought
for tea. It turned out that I had been invited alone, and
this was for discussion. I had tea in the garden, but
Gertrude and Gretchen had none in the house. W. has no
use for social chit-chat.

This was for discussion and so I brought up a
remark of W.'s on Thursday evening. W. had said in
response to my saying that I had read some of *The
Brothers* to show what I meant by "pride," "but a man
might have written a quite different sort of thing." I
wanted to get the point of that. Apparently what he
meant was that pride might be represented as a part of an
heroic scene, and it wouldn't do at all. (I suggested
Andrei seizing the banner at Austerlitz.) In this connection—no, later—he brought up "No man likes to appear
ridiculous." This came up after I was pressed more about
the point of my saying "Pride is an evil." So I had to try
again. I said, well, I came to say it, in some such way as
this. The love of one's neighbor is good. Whatever in us
keeps us from or hinders us in loving our neighbors is
evil. Now, then, what does? Well, pride is such a hin-

drance. Here it was, I think, that he said that no one likes
to appear ridiculous, and this is certainly motivated by
pride, but it helps one to get on with people. I did not see
this clearly at the time, but apparently he meant to
object to the general statement: Pride is a hindrance—

Well, we drifted. What did I do? There were readings: Epicurus, the Stoics, etc. In discussing Epicurus, I
came to ask whether or not we could criticize our
desires. Are there evil desires? Oh, yes, revenge is evil.
The students agreed with me. Well, what of it? What
next? I had no next. How pointless! I was desperate. See, I
said. Solomon said: The love of money is the root of evil.
Pascal said: Most of the troubles of men arise from
this … Now I said, my statement is something like
these. (I could not think of Plato's statement—The love
of luxury is the cause of war …, etc.) How do statements
like these have any meaning? W. said that they did not,
apart from context. Then I said that my sentence is like
G. E. Moore's sentences where Moore answers his question: What things are good? And how about those? Well,
W. was ready for that too. So my sentence was like
Moore's and so what?

It came finally to something like this. I came to
see and admitted that what I do in part is to try to understand what some of these philosophers have said—
Epicurus, Zeno, etc., and to acquaint the students with
this. But I also preach. The first would be on the whole
futile, trifling; the second would be risky. Perhaps it
ought not to be done at all.

All through this W. was talking. He made such
remarks as that some people are interested in a system;
others are interested in preaching. He makes the distinction clear between something up in the air—using his

hands—the talk of philosophers, and now someone saying: Don't be revengeful; let not the sun go down on thy
wrath, etc. This is the distinction between nonsense and
exhortation.

There were also remarks about Dostoyevsky.
Dostoyevsky certainly wanted to preach. But he did not
succeed too well. Notice that Alyosha is represented as
attractive. Smerdyakov is not. This shows a mixed
motive. He has an aesthetic interest in it, too. There was
some puzzling about Dostoyevsky's project: The Great
Sinner. Any decent man might fall into the perpetration
of some crime. Why not?

I have found W. a great tonic, like a purge. And
how I need it. How solid with the habits of long nonsense! I must do what I can to subject myself to his
drubbing and to learn to speak freely so that I may expose
my rags to him. If I can only speak!

August 5

THIS EVENING, after last night's discussion at Black's, W.
came to see me. I have been quite uneasy, overwhelmed,
with W., and here he was coming to see me, and I would
be with him alone. I walked down the street to meet him
and soon he appeared at the corner with his cane and a
rather ungainly, stiff and yet fairly vigorous walk. I
greeted him, saying that he seemed to be a good walker;
curiously such pleasantries he treats seriously. Oh, no.
He was not a good walker at all, etc. Then he soon turned
to me to explain why he had come to see me. He wanted
to talk about our meeting of the night before. Was it any
good and did I get anything out of it? He had talked to

Malcolm in the morning and had asked whether it would
be all right to talk to me about it. As we turned into the
yard, he asked where the road led, and would I like to
walk. I said I would, but proposed we ride, and then I'd
show him. Perhaps we could sit in the car to talk. That
suited him. So we went off. On the way he said he would
like to go to the suspension bridge. There were a few
remarks about the meeting but not much. We parked
near the engineering building and joined the path to the
bridge. As we walked, he began talking, and as his cus-
tom is, he would stop and then talk. He hardly knew
how to tell me. It was absurd, etc. "I am a very vain
person." "The talk wasn't good. Intellectually, it may
have been, but that isn't the point." "My vanity, my
vanity." Here we are talking as though we understood
things, talking, talking. I remember how Alice said that
years ago he had confided in her too that he was unwor-
thy. At any rate, he has his inner struggles. I asked him
after we had crossed the bridge (where the cracks in the
bridge bothered him, made him uncomfortable) whether
such evenings robbed him of his sleep, and he said that
they did not. But then he added in all seriousness and
with the kind of smile Dostoyevsky would suggest in
such a circumstance: "No, but do you know, I think I
may go nuts." This is almost certainly one of his fears.
And he is fearing too his age, his weakness, his poor
health. "You know," he said, "I resigned my position at
Cambridge for two reasons. First I wanted to finish my
book." Then he talked a little about his book—begun
eighteen years ago. "Second, why should I teach? What
good is it for X to listen to me? Only the man who thinks
gets any good out of it." He made an exception of a few
students, who had a certain obsession and were serious.

"But most of them come to me because I am clever, and I am clever, but it's not important. And they just want to be clever." W. had taken me to be his confidant. "So the rope-walker is clever, too."

(Earlier he had also said that science or electronics was aseptic and such talk was, too. But philosophy ....)

We walked along the bridge by the road, and looked over towards the lake, where there was a ball game under the lights. There was an iron floor on the bridge, all holes. He'd never seen a bridge like that. Neither had I. We walked back along the other side of the gorge and sat down on a bench there.

Here he talked to me about his career. He studied engineering at Berlin and Manchester. Got interested in Schopenhauer through his brother. Went to talk with Gottlob Frege at Jena, during which the figure of the cinema lamp in talking about *cogito, ergo sum*, first occurred to him. Studied at Cambridge, heard Bertrand Russell. After the First World War he taught in Austria. It was there that Moritz Schlick invited him for discussions. Later he did go and met with Schlick, Friedrich Waismann, Feigl, and some woman whom he thought Feigl had later married. Then he talked a little about Yorick Smythies. Smythies will never get a lectureship. He is too serious.

As we were walking, he spoke too of the way he worked. He worked in spurts. There were times when he was so dull that he could scarcely believe he had written what he had written. And he had been ill since March, and now for the first time since, he was beginning to do something.

By the time we left our bench, it was dark, and we groped our way back along the path—got off once, going down into the gorge, to the road above the gorge. As we approached the car, he asked me whether I had ever had any acquaintance with the Mormons. They fascinated him. They are a fine illustration of what faith will do. Something in the heart takes hold. And yet to understand them! To understand a certain obtuseness is required. One must be obtuse to understand. He likened it to needing big shoes to cross a bridge with cracks in it. One mustn't ask questions.

Later in the car he mentioned a chapter in Dickens' *Uncommercial Traveler*—an account of Dickens' visit to an immigrant ship of Mormons and his amazement at finding it all so clean, and so orderly and contrary to everything he had expected. The account of a prejudice. I should read it. He also had read a history of the Mormons—Edward Meier. In the midst of this I had mentioned Ivan as wishing he were a woman of eighteen stone lighting a candle before the ikon. This was wrong, of course, not like Dickens at all. But this led him to talk of *The Brothers*. He must have read every sentence there fifty times. Alyosha faded, but Smerdyakov, he was deep. This character Dostoyevsky knew. He was real. Then he said that the book did not interest him much anymore. But to *Crime and Punishment* he should like to return. And he talked about the detail in that book, the house of the murder, the room, the hallway, staircase, etc. But what struck him as most magnificent was Raskolnikov's having forgotten to lock the door. That was tremendous! And after all his planning. (It occurs to me now—like the fly on Pascal's nose.)

(Earlier on the bench, he also said that all the years of his teaching had done more bad than good. And he compared it to Freud's teachings. The teachings, like wine, had made people drunk. They did not know how to use the teaching soberly. Did I understand? Oh, yes, they had found a formula. Exactly.)

Then we rode to the top of the hill near the library and looked over the town. The moon was in the sky. "If I had planned it, I should never have made the sun at all. See! How beautiful! The sun is too bright and too hot." Later, he said, "And if there were only the moon there would be no reading and writing."

It was a memorable evening.

August 6

ROMANS 9:21
"one vessel unto honor; another unto dishonor"
"vessels of wrath"
"vessels of mercy"

ISAIAH 45:9
"For as the heavens are higher than the earth, so are my ways higher than your ways, and my thoughts than your thoughts."

Both of these texts arose in W.'s discussions last evening.

August 7

ON THURSDAY EVENING we met at Black's. It was my turn to introduce the subject. I introduced: *Cogito, ergo sum.* After I had finished, W. took it up. "Of course, if ———— now told me such a thing, I should say: Rubbish! But the real question is something different. How did Descartes come to do this?" I asked, did he mean what leads up to it in Descartes' thinking, and the answer was: "No. One must do this for oneself." Then he went on to discourse. "I always think of it as like the cinema. You see before you the picture on the screen, but behind you is the operator, and he has a roll here on this side from which he is winding and another on that side into which he is winding. The present is the picture which is before the light, but the future is still on this roll to pass, and the past is on that roll. It's gone through already. Now imagine that there is only the present. There is no future roll, and no past roll. And now further imagine what language there could be in such a situation. One could just gape. This!"

Now let me see if I can digest this. I think I see now that this is an interpretation, a way of showing how Descartes' "I think" could seem to him to mean something. If you begin as Descartes does, eliminating everything which his arguments are supposed to render doubtful, then see what goes. There is nothing, no sun, no earth, no fire, no dressing-gown, etc. Of course, these seem to be, there would be seemings. So too there would be no past things, no past earth, no past fire, friends, etc. And no future. Now there is nothing. But there is now something which is comparable to the pictures on the screen. Now a scrupulously honest Descartes will not say: "There goes my horse. Ah! A bird singing up in the tree, etc. There's a woman holding an umbrella." Neither is there, of course, any screen, or man with a machine. So Descartes can present nothing. One can say that he might say: *"Ah!"* or *"This!"* or *"Awareness!"* But if he now said anything of this sort, his words would have no meaning. There would be nothing to provide a contrast. "I think" is or would be like: "Ah!" (uttered by W. leaning forward).

W. then went on with: "I exist." Imagine a lamp on a post. And a light in the lamp. Sometimes there is no light. But go on now to imagine not a light, but a steady succession of lights passing through the lamp-frame. This is James' stream of consciousness. Now one might say: See, there is not only the lights, there is also the lamp. The lamp is the *I* that exists for the lights to pass through. This is something like what Descartes might have imagined.

There were comments and suggestions as we went along, on the past and the future where all is given, on Descartes' treatment of $2 + 3 = 5$, language, etc. W. said: We may compare language to money (counters), but then we think of money in terms of something you can get for it and can carry away—a cabbage, a chair, a cigar, etc. But you can also get a seat at the cinema which you cannot carry away at all.

The latter part of the evening was taken up with a nice question of Black's. He agreed with the disposition of "I think" and "I exist," but he wanted to know what I would do if a student said not: "I think," but "I see something." I went on to say that I would treat it in the same way. At this point W. took it over. The argument was about a very important point. When does a sentence make sense? There was talk about Moore's sentence: I am here. Moore thought one could decide that "I am here" made sense, by some introspective questioning. Does it make sense? Now, of course, all these sentences have a use. The question is whether, if one shouted such a sentence under any circumstances whatever, it has a use. I can see what moves Black. Black says that the sentence obviously has no particular point, nobody gets any information by it. But if it were a question in a True-False questionnaire, you would clearly answer "True" or "Yes" if asked: Yes or No. W. said: "No! No! Of course not, etc. Context determines use."

August 8

ON SATURDAY EVENING the Malcolms and W. were out to dinner, and after dinner Malcolm, W., and I began our discussion in the garden. The subject was determinism and free will. It was a subject I had already discussed with the students on Wednesday evening.

The discussion began much as I had taken it up on Wednesday. We know how we use such expressions as "responsible," "free," and "can't help it," etc. Now the uses of these expressions are quite independent of whether or not there are laws of nature.

I noticed that a part of the difficulty, the puzzle, arises from the use of the word "cause" in the statement of the problem. All my acts are caused—muscles, ligaments, electricity. If my act is caused, then it appears that I am like a clock. And I am. But clocks are not re-sponsible. So if we are all like clocks, then that settles it.

I am not very sure or very clear about this discus-sion. This seems to be it. Holding oneself responsible, holding another responsible—these are attitudes. So the attitude one takes towards a drunk—praising—blaming—is different from that we take toward a sober man who may do what the drunk does. In such cases we might say that it's a difference in chemistry, and one does not blame alcohol. It may be, of course, that in the case of the sober man it's also a matter of chemistry. But when we hold him responsible we suppose that there is a difference. One of the lessons drawn from this is that we should perhaps never judge another. The man may be like the drunkard. But yourself you must judge. Conscience involves this. Calvin, Saint Paul, Romans 9. If you think of man as a pot and of God as the potter, then holding man, the pot, responsible, is what? Then God is responsible? "The sins of the fathers are visited upon the children." W. would not judge.

These are the facts: We do not hold a drunk responsible. The alcohol makes a difference. We do hold the sober man who does what the drunk does, responsible. Who knows, however, that this is not also a matter of chemistry? There may be something in his body which makes the temptation irresistible. It is conceivable that you would not, following some such suggestion, hold any man responsible. You simply would not know whether to hold him responsible or not. So with any man. But each man would now hold himself responsible—not to do this would mean that one would cease to be human. In all these cases we take an attitude. Taking an attitude is blaming, praising, defending, etc. And these are the facts about our attitudes.

And now this is one way in which the problem may be stated further: Would your attitude towards your friend or towards anyone remain the same if when he lies to you, you could have observed the course of electrical impulses over a period of five minutes in slow motion as they culminated in his speaking. Would you still be inclined to blame him? Now imagine that your friend is only a cog or a certain part only of a grand electrical system, Schopenhauer's Will, then would not you contemplate that with horror? It may not now matter that what you see is flowers and birds, or heroic men or bloody villains or men in fear and terror. What would your attitude be? Omar Khayyam: "As impotently moves as you or I."

Kant, as I remember, asked: Can there be uncaused events? and he said: Yes. In this way he made way for freedom. Freedom is possible. This makes the question twofold: Is man free, responsible, guilty, etc.? This is the ordinary sense. The other question is a metaphysical question. Is man free? meaning: Does man cause uncaused events?

It takes some time for the motion of the locomotive to be communicated to the last boxcar.

W. said, I think, that the problem is crucial—he maybe, meant serious and not simply speculative—when in respect to something which you yourself have done, you cannot now make up your mind whether you could help it or not, whether you were responsible. In this case your attitude towards your own self as, I suppose, a small horror, might make you anxious. Here the uncertainty, the problem, invades one's own personality. But I do not now understand this. I need some illustrations. Ivan doesn't know whether he is guilty or not. He decides. I suppose that in respect to the universe or in respect to another human being this question may be left in suspense. But in respect to oneself the issue is suffered, is an agony of spirit. Am I a living horror?

How "must," "had to," "couldn't be otherwise" come to be associated with "cause"? Through the law, and now the use of the law as premise.

If one asks: Are my decisions caused, is there any way of telling?

August 10

YESTERDAY IN THE AFTERNOON I went to Norman's. We had tea and talk in the basement. W. gave a restatement of what he had said on Saturday. First of all there is no opposition between freedom and causality. But there may be a conflict of attitudes towards some person or towards ourselves where, let us say, I have a toothache and am irritable and say things. In any case, as I see it now, the real puzzle is that our attitudes, holding people responsible, praising, blaming, might be quite different from what they are, if we could actually *see* the succession of causes at work. And this is about all there is to say. As it is now, we do have these attitudes. What would our attitudes be if we knew so-and-so? Who knows? We do not praise and blame a man who is drunk, who is insane, etc. If we say that we do not because in these cases we know the causes of the actions, then what if there are causes in all cases, and we know them?

I suggested then the subject of an ideal language in which all the temptations to philosophy would be avoided, but Norman remarked that it would be better to take that up in connection with some problem. So we passed on to reading Frege, W. in his German version.

The subject was: Identity. Is this a relation? And what is a relation? Cousin of, on the table, birds in the tree—etc. Now consider identity where it is the identity of two expressions as these are involved in definition: Herman is Norman. Now this means that these two names are used in the same way. But isn't it curious now to say that there is a relation between them?

Here Norman introduced a puzzle (Moore's about analysis). An oculist is an oculist. W. said: We must

distinguish between the rule for the use of these words
and sentences in which these words are used. In such
sentences such substitution may accordingly be made.
But not in the rule.

This however turned out not to be the issue. The
issue is rather this: In an analysis, the sentence which
you get analyzing sentence *S* is more complex than *S*,
and yet is to mean just what *S* means. There are concepts
in the analyzing sentence which are not in *S*. This is a
puzzle. If we say that they both mean the same proposition, then it appears that two propositions are the same
proposition.

> Norman is 6 feet tall
> Norman is 7 − 1 feet tall

W. first pointed out that if Moore had talked about
sentences instead of propositions, he would have had no
trouble. It is the idea of the proposition as intermediary
which gives the trouble. The intermediary won't help.
"See," W. said, "in this way I can tell you that Norman
has set his cup in his saucer upside down." And he set
his own in his saucer. What I did is like a sentence. But
no intermediary is required. This led us into the question
as to how language works. How are we to understand? A
sentence has meaning or there is the sentence and the
thought. The thought or the meaning is said to be
something. In the case of some words, proper names,
there is commonly something to point to in explaining
the use of the word. This is what misleads. You want to
point to something. In the case of: Norman is 4 feet tall,
there is nothing to point to, but there is *something*—a
proposition. *This is very important!* When we do point to
something to explain, the effectiveness of pointing

depends upon a very complex technique. Suppose
Norman says: "This is W." W. is sitting. Then W. got up.
Is this what he meant? Then he stretched his arms up.
This? Then sideways. This? etc. Then he did something
of the same sort pointing at his cup: "This is Max." What
is Max? And at the plate: "This is red." These operations
are terribly complicated.

"I said in my book: The sentence is the picture."

August 14

CERTAINLY ONE CAN PLAN to do certain things. But so
many things happen which one cannot plan at all. They
are not things one does. They are things which are done
to one or things which happen to one. Perhaps one could
plan to be prepared no matter what happens, prepared to
steel oneself, prepared to give way. Certainly if one sets
great store on or by what one is to do, one must live
precariously. For little mice run away with man's plans.
Perhaps the main point is that no matter what happens
and whether it is planned or not, one cannot plan his
attitudes—hope, fear, joy, despair, etc. And these are
what matter.

On Thursday evening we met at Malcolm's.
Black read some paragraphs from Aristotle's *De
Interpretatione* on necessity, possibility, etc. The
problem turned out to be a problem about the use of
"if-then." W. first distinguished Russell's use of
the expression "material implications" which excludes
but one possibility.

p and not *q* is impossible.

Then he went on to say something about if-then. "If-

then" states a law. Black said: "If I throw this penny in
the next four seconds, it will come up heads—and then I
throw it not. I don't throw it. One might say: See, I told
you." This in any case was supposed to illustrate "if-
then"—no law. W. struggled over this. He said: "There is
a picture here," and then he would pause as though
trying to get the picture. He would begin again and
hesitate. "I am just terribly sorry." Finally he got up, after
making certain abortive suggestions about Providence.
Then he said: "Imagine I'm an invisible engineer. You
who are about to throw the dice see me, and know that I
will be present for four seconds, and will control the fall
of the dice. This is one sort of picture which may go with
your sentence."

This took quite a while. Later we got onto such a
sentence as: If the horse has run, he will have won. This
looks like the past of: If the horse runs, he will win, so
that if the second is true, the first will be true, after the
event. But this is not the case. The second sentence does
not involve any use at all, after the event. The first
sentence has a use, but its use cannot be figured out from
the use of the second. Actually, the first is used only
when we are ignorant of whether or not the condition
has been realized. Once we know, the sentence has
no use.

There was also some talk concerning the
contrary-to-fact conditional: If you had taken the money,
you would now be well. This is the subjunctive, and I
expect is based on the law: If he takes the money, he will
be well. All that is added in this case is the information
that he did not take the money.

Black also wanted to distinguish between the
conditional statement, and the conditioned statement.

This led to such sentences as:

> If he comes, open the door.
> If Malcolm rises to the ceiling, open the door.
> If Wittgenstein grows a beard a yard long, I will too.
> Jump to New York.

The issue turned to this: Is a man giving a command when he knows that the command cannot be executed. Black said he could not. Or, rather: Can a man give a command which cannot be executed? I suggested the case of a man who is commanded to do what he has boasted he can do, but which others believe he cannot do. Malcolm elaborated this into the case of the king who commands the boaster to do the rope trick. He says: "I command you to do the rope trick."

Black was quite confused and suggested what he regarded as a similar sentence: I am the husband of this man. W. preferred to work with the sentence: He is his husband—or something like this.

August 15

UTILITARIANISM:

> "The best for the most"
> Syruptitiously.

Here are some definitions I gave for my logic test:

> Politics is the art of taking from Peter to give to
>   Paul, and getting them both to like it.
> Diligence is having something to do and doing it.
> Knitting is cross-needling with yarn or thread.
> A flirt is a Georgie-Porgie.

A dispute is two people talking loud.
A cheat is a man who smiles while he picks your
    pocket.
Sin is nobody's business.

This afternoon W. talked with us again. He began
again to speak of the temptation to think of an intermediary. Two things tempt us. First there are false
propositions. Here we are likely to talk as though there
must be something else since there is no fact to correspond to the sentence. Second there is this: Even when
there is a fact, we say that along with the sentence there
is a thought.

Now in connection with a sentence there may be
a picture. Whether or not it is in our minds does not now
matter. Imagine that Norman tells me how to go to Mr.
Bouwsma's house. Then I may, as he talks, draw the
route which he describes. So I have a picture. But clearly
I could dispense with the picture. I could simply remember his words as I walked. The words themselves serve
as a picture. The picture I drew is unnecessary.

All this was however introductory. What W.
wished to say was that learning a language is learning a
technique. In understanding the word "raining," we
learn how to compose and how to use all sorts of
sentences containing that word. The technique is
implied in such questions as: What does the word
"raining" mean? A small child cannot ask that question.
A child may when it sees the rain, say "raining," but that
is a different thing. It is merely making a noise.

The whole point of this emphasis upon technique
is to help us to get rid of the common impression that
language is like a mirror, and that whenever a sentence

has meaning, there is something, a proposition, corresponding to it. Using language is exercising a technique.

He said: You cannot know the meaning of any sentence without knowing the whole language. Knowing the whole language means, I think, knowing how it fits in with other sentences, and the permutations of it in respect to tense, modifiers, etc. Is it perhaps the same as the grammar? In any case, words are used, sentences are used, perhaps we should say only sentences are used. Use is technique.

W. tried to explain by the analogy with a map. In a map, squares may represent houses and lines may represent streets, and this now may be explained to a child. This is a house and this is a street. "Now it's as though everything on the map represents something," W. said, but "representing is not represented on the map." The map we may say represents. That it is a map involves that the map is used in a certain way. Its use is what makes it a map. In the same way it is the use of a sentence which makes it intelligible.

When one learns map-reading one learns how to use a certain configuration of marks on a paper. So a map is a certain way of using. And the map does not show one how it is to be used. One must come to it treating it as a map. A map is something to be used in a certain way. And so with sentences.

Get what is implied in this: The meaning of some words may be shown by pointing, but the meaning of a sentence cannot be shown. This once more may be what misleads us. As some words have ostensive definition, so we suppose sentences to. In this way we come to suppose that there are propositions which as it were the sentence points to.

So a map-reader is one who knows how to use maps. And one who speaks a language is one who knows how to use sentences. (Noises, etc.)

W. really struggled to make this point. He considers it extremely important. To understand sounds or marks as a sentence is to be able to use them in a certain way. To say that certain sounds are a sentence is to say that they have a certain use. So too to say that a sheet of paper is a map is to say that it has a certain use. This does strike me as very important. I certainly did not get this this afternoon.

W. went on to read Frege. We struggled over:

"the same meaning" but not "the same sense."
The evening star is the morning star.
The son of Mary is the son of John.
The end of this way through the woods is the same
   as the end of this way through the woods.

The puzzle here lies in the use of these expressions: "same meaning," "same sense." W.'s point in part is that the meaning of a proper name is never an object. For though Mary may die, the meaning of the word "Mary" does not die. But W. was "a stupid ass," and the discussion was ended. "I'm so sorry."

I meant this tree. What tree did you mean? I meant the same tree.

August 17

THIS AFTERNOON W. and I rode out to Taughannock and took the path down the gorge to the falls. W. noticed the leaves again of the tulip tree. He had noticed them before with Norman on Tuesday, and sought out the tree after finding a leaf. And here now were others unsought. We picked a few thimble berries. We also saw some trees which I thought were sycamores but which W. identified as plum trees, white bark, scaling in patches. On the way back we also noticed a caterpillar-like creature, walking along our path on twenty-four short legs, a dark brown tractor with some place to go. W.'s curiosity is wide. He is eager, seeing everything. He was especially intent on identifying a sugar maple. He would break the leaf-stem to find sap. But he failed. Did I know that that was not a sugar maple?

On the way he had begun to talk about the difficulty of discussing Frege, and explained how Frege had come from the problems of math, and now talked and wrote about all sorts of problems without making the proper distinctions. So, pointing to a house along Cayuga Heights Road: The couple who live in that house—well, there may be no such couple. But we know how to find out. We'll stop and see. But in mathematics, there are expressions of the same sort—the least converging series and we may show that there is no such convergent series. But this is not an empirical matter. Frege did not make this sort of distinction. By this time we had gotten into town, and he said maybe I wasn't interested, etc. Then I said that I too had been thinking about Frege's saying that the meaning of two expressions may be the same, although their sense is different, and offered an account of what led Frege to say this. We worked with: The son of Mary is the son of John. When I had finished, he said I was perfectly right, perfectly right—but he added some comment. After an interval— we were driving along—he began again talking about

Frege's original question: Is equality a relation, and
showed how he would deal with it. If you can express
what is meant by a = b, without using the word at
all, dispensing with what gives use to the question—
that will be all that is necessary. It went something like
this: If there is an *a*, then whatever is *a*, is also *b*.
And about this time we got to the falls, where
we walked.

 Walking along he was still thinking of what had
been said before. When someone asks: Who is the son of
Mary? he is not asking how the expression is used. He
knows that. And there was more talk of Frege. Frege is so
good. But one must try to figure out what was bothering
him, and then see how the problems arise. There are so
many of them.

 When we got to the end of the gorge, he wanted
particularly to avoid some women who were sitting
there, and suggested we cross over and sit down on the
rocks. He talked. He was surprised and amused at a
remark of Raymond's. Raymond is twelve. He wondered
whether when people taste something—a lemon—they
taste sour just as he does. Here is philosophy without
artifice. Harmless, for it makes no difference. It has no
consequences. W. wondered whether Norman would go
on and be contented teaching philosophy when he was
older. When he first knew him, he had advised him
against it, and did so often. Later, after he had made up
his mind to it, W. left off. But now? I suggested that W.
himself had not always felt this way about his teaching.
And here I think he wished to make a distinction
between his doing it and somebody else's doing it. He
said that he once had a student—now a lecturer at
————. To him he said: "Now suppose I knew the

truth—white and hot—and could teach it to you. Would it now follow that you too could teach it—now cold or warmed over? Of course not. But the poor fellow is now a teacher, and a very poor one." In any case, now W. could not stand teaching teachers. Those students of his whom he is now fairly certain he did some good, are not philosophers at all. One is a doctor, Dr. Drury in Dublin, and several are mathematicians. He did not mention his otherwise good friends in philosophy. In this way, philosophy, studying it, is simply a course in thinking—clearing away confusions. Once these are cleared away one is prepared for other work.

He made other remarks. This is the age of popular science, and so this cannot be the age of philosophy. He was not objecting to this. In fact he recommended Faraday's *The Chemical History of a Candle* as an illustration of fine popular science. He objected to the sensationalism, and what he called the cheating. Eddington and Jeans cheat. A fine work in this order would have to be very careful; analogies would be well chosen and nicely worked out. In fact the consummation of philosophy might very well be just such fine popular science, work which does not cheat and where the confusions have been cleared up. He was especially resentful of philosophy on the radio—more sensationalism.

On the way back—he has quite a job now getting back on his feet after sitting on a slab of rock—he began talking too about Paul Schilpp's volumes. Perfectly silly! He had never read any of these—had opened the Moore volume—read about Moore's boyhood—very nice, but the shoemaker also had a boyhood, very nice. Dewey—

was Dewey still living? Yes. Ought not to be. Russell was once very good. Once did some hard work. Cambridge kicked him out when he was good. Invited him back when he was bad. Russell lectured in 1945—three auditoriums full of women and American soldiers. The last lecture was on Russell. It was dreadful, horrible. But when W. had first come to Cambridge, Russell was fine in discussion. Saw Russell last about three years ago at Moral Science Club. Passed each other but did not speak. No profit. He knew A. N. Whitehead too, and discussed with him. Very good before he became a charlatan.

He wondered what happened to such men. They do good work for some years, hard work. They have talent too, especially Russell. But then it's as though they said: "I've done enough." Then they relax. They do philosophy. This has happened to other men in science too. They rest, coast, do philosophy. Hertz, he mentioned, as one who did not relax.

As I look back upon these talks, it strikes me more and more that W. is a thoroughly honest man, whose conception of good work he carries through with rigor. In terms of it he keeps the reins tight on himself, and what is more striking perhaps, he is merciless in his judgement of others. This is, at least, in part what motivates his scorn and his unrelenting severity in respect to all who have pretensions. He does know how to judge, and is sensitive to all shoddiness and cheating. No wonder he has enemies. He cannot suffer fools gladly. What surprises me is his patience and his friendliness towards me. Perhaps he sees that I do have no pretensions—at least not in his presence.

August 20

TODAY, SATURDAY, Norman and W. came about four o'clock for discussion. The subject was Moore's: "I know that this is a hand." And the background was Norman's article and Moore's letter. Norman proposed the question: What view is it that Moore is opposing? It is, of course, some view which involves the denial that Moore knows this is a hand, some form of idealism, or skepticism.

W. began by distinguishing the nature of the sentences which are used in a physics laboratory, and those which are used in a psychological laboratory. Sentences of the latter type are such as these: This looks yellow. There appears to be— There seems—, etc. Such sentences as these permit of no doubt. To doubt them makes no sense. I doubt that this seems yellow—is without sense. This is now not true of the sentences in the other class. It may make sense to say: I doubt that there is a light there. But not that this sentence is doubtful. If now the first type of sentence is regarded as a kind of standard, this is knowledge, then obviously one never "knows" any sentence of the other type to be true. And this now leads some philosophers to talk about all such sentences as: This is a hand, This is a tree, etc., as hypotheses.

So we get this gradation of sentences:

This appears yellow.
This is yellow.
The moon is spherical.

and a fourth, which should be third:

This is a hand.

The gradation is unmistakable, and now it may be clear that: the moon is spherical, is an hypothesis, and so also is: This is a tree.

I am not sure about all this, but a part of what is meant with respect to the sentence "The moon is spherical" being an hypothesis, is that one can never see that it is a sphere. One sees only a face. It might be a cylinder or a cone, etc., or like a disc. This is how: The moon is spherical, is different from: The ball is spherical. The difference in the sort of game in which it enters is what is meant by its being an hypothesis. A part is seen but another part is not seen and cannot be seen.

In trying to make this plain, W. tried such analogies as these: You would have something like an hypothesis about what is in this room, if you gave a list and then added: "and a rabbit which disappears whenever anyone looks." What makes it like the hypothesis is that something is now included which no one can see. Or imagine: There is a chair in here which grows a protuberance when nobody is present, and it disappears when anyone comes. If you had sentences like this, then you might say that you were maintaining an hypothesis. The point, of course, is that sentences like: This is a chair, This is a tree, etc., are not hypotheses at all. W.'s point is that the difference is not clearcut, is a matter of gradations, and that this is what leads to the trouble.

Now then is Moore simply pointing out here that: This is a hand, This is a tree, etc., is not an hypothesis? This approach did not turn out to be very fruitful in relation to Moore's sentence.

So W. returned to Moore's sentence. A man squinting, closing one eye, might say:

X: I don't know about this and I don't know about this, but I know this is a tree.

Y: What is it?

X: That's a tree.

Y: That's what you say, but you don't know.

X: We'll see.

They walk in the direction of what they saw. Then:

X: Now, how do I know that's a tree?

Here the contrast is between just saying that's a tree, and knowing that's a tree. In the first case it's between the case in which you try to distinguish and fail, and that in which you try and succeed.

What W. tries to do is to consider uses of the phrases in Moore's sentence in order to show either that they do or do not have an ordinary sense. What is the ordinary sense? Ordinary sense can be seen only in examples. This must be brought out in order to compare Moore's sentence. One must see this difference.

W. got interested in the use of "this" in "this is a hand," "this is a tree." Here again he imagined. He squinted, looking across the rug. "What is this?" He threw down a package of cigarettes. Again: "What is this?" Now "this" doesn't mean: a package of cigarettes, and "this" need not mean a physical object. "This" may mean: What I am seeing. What is this I'm seeing? It may be a package of cigarettes, a shadow, or the play of light on the floor. So he walks over, picks it up: "It's a package of cigarettes." Of course, one may say: "What is that on the table?" meaning: "I can see there's something on the table, but what is it?"

Again he stood up. Imagine this as a game. He went to his chair and said: "Here is a chair," (turning)

"Here is a vase," "Here is a lamp"—then he turned about to go into the dining room, "And now I advance into the next room and go on drawing my map of this room. This also shows how these expressions fit into a situation." A way which is forbidden to man himself. Surely God instructs man, but as a man can be instructed.

What is the difference between the feeling and attitude towards the world as between that of the atheist and the believer? Here I am echoing something of John Wisdom's. Atmosphere! Hope! Promise! More! Glory! and now, it's all given, you see what there is, that's all, nothing wonderful, nothing terrible! Just so-so.

August 22

TODAY I WALKED AGAIN WITH W. above the gorge at Taughannock.

On the way as we passed the Jewish synagogue, he remarked that he did not understand modern Judaism. He did not see what could be left of it since sacrifice was no longer practiced. And now? What was left was too abstract. Prayers and some singing. Later I suggested that in Zionism there was perhaps some intention to restore the temple and the old rites. He thought very few. Jews had no such interest.

Later on our walk I suggested that from what he had said it must be that with the destruction of the temple the head of Judaism was gone. Now nothing is left but the body. But he checked me. The spirit may have gone out long before this. And even after this sects, very strict sects, most likely contrived. The passing of Greek religion illustrates the same point. I was reminded of the allegorizing of Greek myth. But W. protested he was perhaps talking rubbish. In any case a religion is bound up with a culture, with certain externals in a way of life, and when these change, well, what remains?

Then he went on to cite the Oxford Movement as a symptom of the same hollowness, lifelessness, in the Anglican church. I didn't understand all these things. I suppose that the point is that once the sacrifices, whatever there was in Greek religion, and the ceremonies and ritual in Anglicanism, were entered into with earnestness and serious intent, with spirit. At a later time, they were done listlessly, mechanically, and as unessential. Once this happens it is finished. But religion without ceremony, without ritual—this is impossible. W. stresses here, I think, the precise forms and practices, the very words to be spoken—creeds, sacraments, etc.

Later he asked me, had I read Newman? He was much impressed by Newman. Kingsley accused him of insincerity. But Newman was sincere. He, W., had read *Grammar of Assent* too. That was puzzling. How a man of such learning and culture could believe such things! Newman had a queer mind.

Later I pressed him for an explanation. Did he mean by "queer" that a man like Newman should have become a Roman Catholic? Oh, no. My best friends and the best students I had are converts. What is queer about Newman is the kind of reasons he gives for becoming a Roman Catholic. On miracles, Newman cites the case of Christians, who taken by savages had their tongues cut out, and yet they could speak. He gives a natural explanation for this—if the tongue is only half cut off a man cannot speak, but if wholly cut off a man still can—but Newman then goes on to say that it may nevertheless have been a miracle. Again: The pope excommunicated Napoleon. Napoleon said he didn't care so long as his soldiers' weapons did not fall out of their hands. Some years later in Moscow, in Russia, this is literally what happened.

What was Newman doing? He argued that miracles occur still? How? What God has done once he contrives to do—usually. This is the sort of thing that is so queer in Newman.

Later when we were sitting he remarked that twenty years ago he would have regarded Newman's action as incomprehensible, as insincere perhaps. But no more. When I prodded him about this, what changed him, he pondered, and then he said that he came gradually to see that life is not what it seems. He was quiet for several minutes. Then he said: It's like this: In the city, streets are nicely laid out. And you drive on the right and you have traffic lights, etc. There are rules. When you leave the city, there are still roads, but no traffic lights. And when you get far off there are no roads, no lights, no rules, nothing to guide you. It's all woods. And when you return to the city you may feel that the rules are wrong, that there should be no rules, etc.

This did not enlighten me much. Later as we were walking he said: "It comes to something like this. If you have a light, I say: Follow it. It may be right. Certainly life in the city won't do." I think I understand this. And I think I understand too something about that earlier figure. The city is the life of external action. Here we have simple guides. But outside the city there is the wilderness of nature, desires, emotions. And now what shall we do? And isn't the city a superficial place?

Later as he was sitting on the ledge—which made me very uneasy, for he was very infirm and had a hard time of it getting to his feet again—he began speaking of my plans—Northampton, England, etc....

Then he began talking about how bad philosophy-talk and teaching are. I know what he has in mind. When he says this.... W. had himself talked about philosophy as in certain ways like psychoanalysis, but in the same way in which he might say that it was like a hundred other things. When he became a professor at Cambridge he submitted a typescript to the committee. Keynes was a member of the committee. Of 140 pages, 72 were devoted to the idea that philosophy is like psycho-analysis. A month later Keynes met him and said he was much impressed with the idea that philosophy is psycho-analysis. And so it goes.

A man has a certain way of thinking. It fascinates some people. So he tries to teach it to them. But what can he do? They stay with him two years and so they hear what he says during those years. But this is only a chapter in the long process of his thought. Now they leave him and they want to go further. But they cannot go further. And now what happens? They may use what they have heard as a rigamarole or they may give up and feel cheated. They cannot carry on. And the teacher is stuck. He fails.... Freud, of course, also did incalculable harm, much as W. himself has done....

He also spoke of W. E. Johnson. Johnson always wanted to explain to W. what W. was not interested in. What W. wanted explained, Johnson could not explain. So W. would ask a question, and Johnson would answer a different one, one he could answer. He'd talk about the syllogism. Later W. came to know Johnson much better, a deep man and with a deep love of music too. So they talked about music. And he was so delighted to have

someone agree with him. About a color, for instance.
He never came to Moral Science Club.

Moore lectured and puzzled endlessly, but it was
futile. W. stood it for two terms.

J. M. E. McTaggart he saw once at a squash [i.e., a
reception] at McTaggart's. Came with Russell. Russell
badgered McTaggart about his argument for immortality
of the soul. McTaggart answered, but W. understood not a
word of it.

"Of course, a man need not argue his religious
beliefs. Newman did. Once he does this he must argue
clearly—soundly. But one may believe without
argument."

And so we got back to the car, down by way of the
road—not by the path above the gorge.

August 28

ON THURSDAY AFTERNOON W. and I went for a walk
exploring the falls at Taughannock. He loved it. "This is
the finest walk you've taken me on."

On the way he asked me what we had discussed
the evening before, and I told him: "I ought" implies "I
can." As his manner is, he started out immediately. He
said he thought that the Christian orthodox position was
that this was not so. "Be ye perfect." Still someone in
deep earnest had said to him: But it is commanded. So it
must be possible. Now "possible" or "can" has two
different contexts: It is not possible to grow pears on an
apple tree. This only means that there is a law, and the
law says simply that apples grow on apple trees and pears
grow on pear trees. And if someone makes a chemical

analysis of the apple tree and of the pear, and now says: "So it is impossible," this is really no different. There is simply another law. On the other hand, "I can," "It is possible," means something like: "I'll try" or "I'm still trying," just as "I can't" means: "I give up." One tugs at something to lift it and finally says: "I can't," and this means I give up. Now when it comes to: "Be humble," there is no law. And one may try. That man cannot is more like a prophecy and the prophecy is that man cannot be humble, not that one cannot try. So the command in such cases may imply, not: "I can" but "I can try." So one can try to be humble.

Later when I pointed out that trying to be humble may not be clear at all in the way in which trying to lift a weight is, he said: You are completely right—then he went on with an analogy: It may be something like the doctor who does not pretend he can cure you, but he tells you to rest and not to eat certain foods, and sit in the sun—and as for the rest nature must do the work. So too, though he did not develop this, a priest might say: "Read the scriptures, say your prayers down on your knees, watch yourself—and God must do the rest."

On our walk we did not talk much. A forest of sumacs delighted him and he asked the name of some tall stalks which in German are called King's candles. I didn't know. He loved the scene from the bridge, wanted to know why the cars blew their horns below. He said that though there was room enough on the bridge he would be terrified if a train should pass while we were on the bridge. He was reminded of Kolya [in *The Brothers Karamazov*]. He also scrambled down a steep height, a narrow stony path, clinging to twigs and branches on the way down—he with his neuritis and only one good arm, encumbered too with his cane. Game!

He did speak of all the harm philosophers do in ethics. When a man is in deep earnest about what he ought to do then one can see how fantastic what philosophers do, is. We had a very pleasant time.

On Friday afternoon I took him to the doctor. Afterwards I asked him to have a dish of ice cream and he was glad to. Just before we sat down to our dishes he began remarking about the changes in our way of life since the days of his parents in Vienna. "They would scarcely recognize this as the same world." It is the machines of course which are so obvious. But he had in mind certain changes in the kind of human beings we are, incidental to all these changes in our surroundings. There was a time when our lives were furnished rather simply, a house, a place, tools so many, a beast, and a circle of people. In this simplicity and this stability one grew attached to a limited environment. This gave a life a certain quality—roots. Now not only are people transient, but neighborhoods do not remain the same. We live in surroundings to which we are not sentimentally attached. Most of what we use and own can be replaced by something just as good. He had once heard John Dewey talk about the kind of human being he wished by education to produce. "But I was a human being which was fitted into the old environment." How could he make such a human being in an altogether different environment?

On the way out he was interested in the jukebox. Juke! What's that word? We talked about the bicycle— when was it invented? I remembered my father riding one before 1910. Early French models. He talked about his father's first automobile about 1900.

W. was born in 1889.

On Saturday afternoon—after the morning and picnic at Taughannock—I met with Malcolm and W. It was my privilege to suggest a subject. I suggested that we discuss the difficulties involved in attempts to define "good."

W. sat back and considered. Then he began. Suppose that a certain people (the Jews, perhaps) have a prophet and he lays down the law to them: "Thou shalt not ..." etc. Now the people either obey such laws or when they do not, they feel guilty. No one questions the authority of such laws. Here no one asks: "What is meant by good?" or "What kinds of things are good?" They all say: "So and so is a good man. He keeps the law. Such another is a bad man. He disobeys." But now imagine another reformer-prophet arises and he lays down another law. He wins a following. And now comes another and another. In this process the authority of all law is shaken. Now some men may be bewildered and shaken, and may quite sincerely ask: "What is good? What must I do?" But W. hesitated. Would someone in such a case ask for a definition? If he asked for a definition, to what end would he do this? Guidance? How could it guide him? W. pointed out—he worried over this for some time—that in order for it to serve him, it would have to do so as a resolution by which he would come to alter attitudes. (Good is whatever is conducive to the general welfare.)

Definition of good? What would one do with this? Law courts have a use for definitions. Physics has a use for definition. It is hard in any case to see what a definition here could be like. What one can do is describe certain aspects of the uses of the word "good." If you start out with "X is good" means "I approve of X"—well this is a common part of most uses of the word. But the use is infinitely complex. The use of a word in such a case is like the use of a piece in a game, and you cannot understand the use of a queen unless you understand the uses of the other pieces. What you do with one sort of piece is intelligible only in terms of what you do with it in relation to what is done with the other pieces. So the word "good" is used in a terribly complex game, in which there are such other pieces as "ought to do," "conscience," "shame," "guilt," "bad," etc. And there are now no strict rules for the use of any and yet the uses are interdependent. Even such phrases as: "I approve" or "Someone approves" might not always apply. *I* approve but the law says so and so—a good Jew might say this.

Consider the use of the word "good" in the nursery and in the school, when we use it to encourage, as a part of moral training. Contast this use with that in the New Testament or in the Old. Here we find: "Why callest me good?" At one point W. was asking whether it made any sense to speak of "good in the Christian sense." He finally decided that it did not unless it meant "good by Christian standards," which is something else.

Towards the end of our discussion which had lasted several hours, W. spoke of A. C. Ewing's definition—in a Moral Science lecture, "Good is what it is right to admire." Then he shook his head over it. The definition throws no light. There are three concepts, all of them vague. Imagine three solid pieces of stone. You pick them up, fit them together and you get now a ball. What you've now got tells you something about the

three shapes. Now consider you have three balls of or
lumps of soft mud or putty—formless. Now you put the
three together and mold out of them a ball. Ewing makes
a soft ball out of three pieces of mud.

Here is another formulation of the issue. Imagine
a tribe who when they viewed things that were horrible,
loathsome to us, clapped their hands, their faces bright,
and now they always uttered the word "doog." And now
you are to translate the word "doog." How will you
translate it? Will you hesitate about this? W. was trying
here to bring out the unsatisfactory character of "I
approve." The tribe apparently approves. Will "good"
do? I suppose that this involves that the use of the word
"good" is affected in some such way as this: That in
reference to "good" the use of the word "good" comes to
serve also in naming the things that are good. One might
be horrified not simply at people's regarding such things
good but also at their calling them good. Simply perhaps
this. If we were to translate "doog" into "good," we
should be suggesting not simply that they approve of
certain things but also that these things are justified by
our law, etc.

Plato's *Euthydemus, Protagoras, Philebus,
Republic.*

The use of the word "good" is too complicated.
Definition is out of the question.

O.K. Bouwsma in the early 1950s.

Smith College

October 11, 1949

WITTGENSTEIN HAS BEEN WITH US now for two days. Monday evening we went to Springfield to meet him and to bring him to Northampton. He is quite weak but still exceedingly keen and vigorous intellectually.

Yesterday about noon we went for a ride to Mount Tom reservation. On the way up he began talking about teaching ethics. Impossible! He regards ethics as telling someone what he should do. But how can anyone counsel another? Imagine someone advising another who was in love and about to marry, and pointing out to him all the things he cannot do if he marries. The idiot! How can one know how these things are in another man's life?

45

I suggested: No man is wise from another man's woe, nor scarcely from his own. But he said: "Oh, no, not quite that. I can only imagine a teacher who is in some way higher than those he teaches and who suffers with those in respect to whose sufferings he is to give counsel." (Who was this teacher, but Jesus Christ?) And the taught must confess to him the innermost secrets of his life, holding nothing back. This would be teaching in ethics.

Later as we stopped on the hill looking down over the city, he asked me: Had I read any Kierkegaard? I had. He had read some. Kierkegaard is very serious. But he could not read him much. He got hints. He did not want another man's thought all chewed. A word or two was sometimes enough. But Kierkegaard struck him almost as like a snob, too high, for him, not touching the details of common life. Take his prayers. They left him unmoved. But he once read the prayers and meditations of Samuel Johnson. They were his meat. "The violent incursions of evil thoughts." (I'm not sure about his judgment here of Kierkegaard.)

Later, walking in the hills, he returned to the way in which we borrow—hints. He had seen a play, a third-rate, poor play, when he was twenty-two. One detail in that play had made a powerful impression upon him. It was a trifle. But here some peasant, ne'er-do-well says in the play: "Nothing can hurt me." That remark went through him and now he remembers it. It started things. You can't tell. The most important things just happen to you.

On the way home he asked me whether I had ever read the letter of François Fénelon to the French Academy, against their purist rules. Admit other words, if only they are sweet. Sweet! How is sweetness judged?

Later he spoke of a friend of his who was an Esperanto enthusiast. *He* couldn't stand it. A language without any feeling, without richness. Strange, he said. Like a man's being offended, repelled by another man's spittle.

This is a fine illustration of the richness of his mind. For all this came about through what? Through seeing a sign advertising "cheeseburgers." That offended him! He loathed it. That was no way to derive words. And what happens? Fénelon.

The vigor, the clarity, the resource! He is a fountain.

That evening at the table Gretchen told about some of her classes, her French, her history, her Shake-speare. W. immediately sees through what is happening and is seriously concerned. She should be learning a few facts in history, not ideas and ideals, centuries! And for Shakespeare he hasn't much use. Some for Lear. Such vigor again, and such concern.

After dinner he looked at her French book. It too was all wrong. The exercises were thoroughly unsuit-able. What foreigner coming to France would say: "Hello, old man!" She should learn her grammar and some simple French in reading. Molière's *Le Médicin malgré lui*. He seems so generally to get things right.

How he hated Truman—a new low. "The Sermon on the Mount! Indeed, that crook, that gangster. And telling the journalists to read it. Awful!"

He talked about his sister in New York and his mother, a fine musician, but she had no patience. He has a brother in New York, a pianist, whom he did not even expect to see. One of eight children.

How do you pronounce Van Gogh? How do you pronounce "gas"? Some Dutchman had coined that word and W. was pretty sure it was derivative by similarity from the word "chaos." He is very likely right, I should think.

He also talked about having spent two weeks as a nurse at the bedside of a nephew injured in a motorcycle accident. He and an old German woman servant took turns. This was in Roermond, Holland. There were the finest nurses he had ever met. Catholic nurses, sleepless for days, yet diligent and cheerful. This again struck him, I could tell, like the Mormons, people who are moved by faith. They've got something.

On Tuesday W. and I walked through the greenhouses and again he showed his amazing interest and knowledge. He thought the place not well kept and that the labels were not well placed. He wanted to speak to someone about it. We saw the banana trees with bananas high and the great green stalk and the flower; and the coffee tree and a Brazil rubber plant about which he was doubtful. He had never seen the moon flower. Afterward we walked along the path to Paradise Pond. He was quite weak and we sat down on a stump there. I felt quite at ease with him. . . . I asked him whether (taking up a hint of his on Monday) teaching consisted of giving hints. He hesitated. He distinguished good hints and bad, and then he pointed out that one gives hints only to people who are looking for something, to people who are eagerly set to follow a hint. Then I asked him whether the pursuit of philosophy required any special gifts. At first he was sure not. What is required is a passionate interest and one that does not fail. . . . A philosopher is someone with a head full of question marks. This seemed to him the essence. He rather enjoyed the question, I think. He went on. Moore is a man who is full of questions but he has no talent for disentangling things. It is one thing when you have a tangle of thread to lay it down that some threads run so: = and some: ‖ and some: ⟍ but it is quite another thing to take an end and follow it through, pulling it out, and looping it on, etc. Moore could not do this. He was barren. Now Russell was different in his good days. He was wonderful. W. did not explain this talent any further. Later on he talked about Whitehead. Whitehead was good once too, before he became high priest, charlatan. The First World War ruined him. During that war W. had corresponded with Russell and asked to be remembered to Whitehead. But Russell never said a word about Whitehead. After the war Russell explained that he could not mention W. to Whitehead because W. was Teutonic, spoke German, etc. The war ruined so many people. Then he went on to talk of another incident which took place in Cambridge after the war. There had been at Cambridge an Hungarian student who when war broke out was sent home. He was killed as an Hungarian soldier. When now the war was ended a plaque was to be erected, set in the wall, with the names of all those who had died for their country. This man's name was on the list too. There was a meeting about it. And who now should protest this name in the list but the Professor of Ethics! So there is now at Cambridge, in Christ Chapel, a plate bearing the name of this Hungarian student, set off by itself, away from all the rest. In death!

He talked about this almost at the end of the walk, when we turned back.

He had also spoken of Moore. When he was in Norway and Moore came to visit him, for two weeks, he had once fallen into a terrible rage with him. This was provoked by Moore's not understanding that W. was writing. Moore is so naive. W. said that when he goes to see him now he (W.) is inexpressibly sad, just hopeless, and can scarcely say a word. Yet he is fond of Moore. The last time he went with Georg Henrik Von Wright and that made it quite easy.

He spoke of Gilbert Ryle. Ryle had been good when he was young. Now he just borrowed other men's thoughts. I suggested that this was due to the burden of administrative duties. But W. said it was much worse.

He spoke on Tuesday of his great surprise at having seen the northern lights in Ithaca—so far south! In Norway he had seen, but there they were all colors in the sky—some bright red.

On Wednesday—no, Tuesday—W., shaking his head over Plato and teaching ethics, was trying to figure out what he could make of it. First he said: "Now when it comes to those early dialogues, one on courage for instance, one might read and say, 'See, see, we know nothing!' This would, I take it, be wholesome." Later he thought of the description of Socrates as outwardly a monster and all beauty within. (This he referred to the *Phaedrus*, but I think he meant the *Symposium*). Of this, he said: "Now there is something which I think I understand."

He says that he scarcely reads any more, but how he did read once! (St. Augustine under the fig tree!)

October 24

IT HAS JUST OCCURRED TO ME this evening what it is about teaching ethics that made him shake his head so. The serious problem in ethics is asked by a man who has some terribly important decision to make: What shall I do? Perhaps the matter becomes ethical just at the point when the question or the decision is felt to be serious or important. What is serious or important in this way?

Bouwsma (left) at Oxford

Oxford

August 17, 1950

LEAVING THERE I WALKED ALONG THE HIGH and cut through by way of Radcliff and the Broad. I walked along and cut through from Beaumont to Wellington Square, but walked back since I did not see how to get through. Walking along Walton Street, whom should I see sitting on a bench but W. He was a surprise since I thought he was in Norway. He is still not very well, but says he is better than he was a year ago. We exchanged a little talk and he seems very friendly. He is going to bring me to see Smythies who works in a forestry library and who, he says, is a good thinker. Weekends, Smythies reserves for his privacy and his thinking, and W. does not see him at all then. I am to see him, W. that is, this afternoon....

Will you lecture much? No. Good.

August 28

Today I walked with W.—along the canal and under the willows. I am thoroughly exhausted.

As we walked, he said that if there was something I should like to talk about I should bring it up. I suggested that some professor was to lecture on: the nature of religious truth—what would he say? Religious truth? He went on puzzling, thinking his way. Of course it isn't botany, it isn't anything about eclipses, it isn't economics or history. That is clear enough. Negatively it is easy to say something. But what is one to say besides that? The man in Christ Church will very likely talk about Christian dogmas. And one might make some sense in this way, each believer talking about what he believes. But there is no sense talking about religious truth in general. What religious? What truth? To illustrate this he cited a story of Gottfried Keller's about a young man and woman in conversation. The young woman told about her falling in with three women who lived together in a small house. The one woman lived by herself in one room, by herself, could get along with no one, was hard and mean. The two lived in the other room and were noted for their sweetness and kind natures. They were also pious, went to church regularly, etc. She—the young woman—once made bold to enquire into the secret of their lives. And they told her, giving her a dry account of what one must believe—something like the Apostle's Creed. The young woman was disappointed. The conversation ends with the young man's saying: "This is my religion—the consciousness, the recognition—that I am at present doing well but that it may not always be so."

This, according to W., was actually Keller's view, his
religion. Keller had apparently been brought up a
Christian—Zwingli, perhaps—and later was interested
in Feuerbach. So this was the shrunken, truncated
Christianity.

Now then if this is religion, what will the man at
Christ Church say about it? For see how much this is
like what is said—namely that religion is man's sense of
dependence. For although this is "nonsense," one can see
how one would come to say this. This is all it is in some
cases and is a part of it in most cases. Schleiermacher
was a serious man and not stupid, and Keller too was "a
deeply grounded religious" man.

I suggested that one would not gather this merely
from this sentence of Keller's. He allowed this and when
I asked whether he spoke of Keller's being serious in the
same way that he spoke of some other men's being
serious, he explained. He meant by serious a man who
endured conflict and struggle, who came back again and
again to these matters. He wrestled. This is not too plain
to me.

The point is, in any case, that religion takes many
forms, there are similarities, but there is nothing common among all religions.

I asked him for an explanation of the sentence:
God is a spirit.

Well, first it means that God is not a human
being, or like a tree. He cannot be seen, heard, etc. At
first it seemed to him that this was all. Then it occurred
to him that one might also say these things about a
number. But one would not say that a number was a
spirit. One means further then that God sees, hears

prayer, forgives, speaks, etc. He allowed that he did not understand. The Gospel of John bothered him. But he was not criticizing. But if someone said that he did understand, then such a one must give an account. Let a man surrender and admit that he doesn't understand.

I quoted the rest of the sentence: "And they that worship him must worship him in spirit and truth." Of course, this meant that man must not worship in mere words and forms without any fervor. I suggested that it involved a rebuke to those who supposed that God was to be worshipped only in a certain place. He objected to this. "Rebuke? How could it be a rebuke? The Jews were taught to worship in a certain place. And, Jesus said he came not to destroy the law, but to fulfil."

("This was to Nicodemus, wasn't it?" I didn't know. Anyhow, Saint John.)

Believe whatever you can. I never object to a man's religious beliefs, Mohammedan, Jew, or Christian. (To the Samaritan woman.)

A peculiarity of religious beliefs is the great power they have over men's lives.

(*Not lehrt uns Beten.*) [Misery teaches us to pray.]

Later as we sat on the bench near the bridge he asked me what I would do in lectures. I made the suggestion about Plato's theory of ideas. He took it up. Ideas! Patterns! He thought this notion of patterns— Jews—Englishmen—Germans—as quite natural as an account of thought, but not as an account of real thinking. Goethe once thought he had come upon the type of all plants.

He came along with me to dinner....

He also said that he had been approached by Ryle

to give the John Locke lectures, but there would have
been an audience of two hundred and no discussion. He
wouldn't do it. People would hear and make something
cheap of what he had said. He might do something for a
group of friends.

September 9

W. SAYS that he doesn't understand everything. He says
this particularly speaking of religious languages. This
now may mean any of several things. It may mean
something like: "I have no use for such language. I
cannot pray." He once said, I remember, that he could
make nothing of the dogma of the Incarnation. And the
Gospel of John puzzles him. He does not "understand"
it. But he does not say that some other people do not
understand it. The question then is about *their* use of
these sentences. And here one thing is clear. Whatever
this use is, it is different from the use of ordinary
sentences describing the world. But this difference then
must be recognized by both those who have a use for
them and by those who do not. Those who have no use
for them are not to disparage all use of them simply
because they cannot deal with them as they deal with:
"Pussy says meow." But likewise those who have use for
them are not to resort to proofs and evidence as they too
might with: "Pussy says meow." But neither will it do
to suggest as Waismann seems to, that this language is
vague. For there is here no contrast with some other
language which is clear. But I hadn't better attribute this
to Waismann. Of course there are religions which are

frankly anthropomorphic. The Greeks certainly did
believe that there was a company of man-like crea-
tures—taller—stronger—more handsome, etc.—who
lived up there on Mount Olympus.

September 14

YESTERDAY AFTERNOON while I was asleep in Gretchen's
room, W. came up. I had been a little uneasy thinking he
wouldn't bother about me. I am unaccountably stupid
when I am with him. He wanted to go for a walk. I still
can't figure out why he would walk with me. Perhaps he
realizes how much I appreciate his talk. We cut through
from Merton Street to the meadows and walked there....
    Philosophers can be so bad—I suspect that W.
looks upon so many of these young philosophers as
beasts of prey and he does not intend to be rabbit to
anyone. But what am I?
    I told him that I was puzzling these days about
hedonism. The hedonist says: "Men desire nothing but
pleasure." As his manner was, is, he does not take nor
use any time to consider. "Obviously this is no empirical
proposition. The hedonist does not find this out by going
about asking people what they want. He has no statistics
about this. And yet he knows very well that people want
all sorts of things. So it isn't at all like: Everybody wants
a motorcar. If someone wants a motorcar, then he wants
pleasure, and if he wants to smoke or to write a letter,
then he wants pleasure. Pleasure is another word for
whatever anyone wants. In other words it's a tautology.
Everyone prefers the preferable. So pleasure is the desir-
able, the preferable.

"But there is, of course, the illusion of having
discovered something. How does that happen? Perhaps
in some such way as this. Freud asked—in his own
language: What is the essence of the dream? Then he
inspected and noticed that a certain dream was a wish-
fulfilment dream. And another, and another. This was it.
A man is hungry and dreams of feasting, is thirsty and
dreams of drinking, feels the need of passing water and
he dreams of passing water. Some dreams are like this.
This comes like a flash, a great light—an *aperçu*. This is
the dream, this is what the dream is fundamentally, its
essence. This is a generalization, and the clarity and the
fascination of the one case deludes one. All dreams are
like this. Now this may be what happens in the case of
the hedonist. For we do sometimes desire pleasure. So
this may be the electrifyingly clear case of desire. There
may, for instance, be cases in which you do not or cannot
say whether you want something for something else or
not—supposing you have brought up the question. Concerning pleasure there is no doubt. Pleasure is desired
and there is no question of 'Why?' or 'For what?' about it.
When it is desired, the case is clear. And now the
temptation is to say that when you desire an automobile,
what you desire is automobile-pleasure, eating-pleasure,
writing-pleasure, etc. The generalization, which was
mistaken at the outset, compels this manner of speaking.
    "Now when, as in the case of Freud, a generaliza-
tion is seized upon, and now investigation continues,
qualifications are introduced. Dreams are not simply
wish-fulfilment, they are *fundamentally* or *in essence*
wish-fulfilment. Classifications are introduced. There
may be clear wish-fulfilment, not so clear, dark wish-

fulfilment, etc. And so with hedonism. Pleasures are not all of the same kind. There are higher and lower. This is the mistake of the generalization breaking out into curious distinctions, or it proceeds to develop the absurdities of the calculus. We desire nothing but pleasure, but there are qualities of pleasure. Poetry-pleasure is better than pushpin pleasure."

(I must make a point of noticing the *aperçu*. Perhaps most proverbs are like that—snappy generalizations.)

About this time we sat on a bench and he began to talk about reading Plato. Plato's arguments! His pretence of discussion! The Socratic irony! The Socratic method! The arguments were bad, the pretense of discussion too obvious, the Socratic irony distasteful—why can't a man be forthright and say what's on his mind? As for the Socratic method in the dialogues, it simply isn't there. The interlocutors are ninnies, never have any arguments of their own, say "Yes" and "No" as Socrates pleases they should. They are a stupid lot. No one really contends against Socrates. Perhaps Plato is no good, perhaps he's very good. How should I know? But if he is good, he's doing something which is foreign to us. We do not understand. Perhaps if I could read Greek!

As for his arguments, they're too formal, too neat. There's no groping. It's X or Y or Z. It's not X, not Y. So: Z. When you're looking for something you go and look closely, if you think D is in a certain place, and if it isn't there you look somewhere nearby. You don't go from X and run over somewhere to Z (pointing back over his head). (This no doubt has something to do with the difference between Plato's conception of the Ideas, and W.'s own notion of family resemblances.) Plato's view

involves this discreteness of ideas: *X* or *Y* or *Z*. W.'s is
more like: *X* or not quite *X* or a little bit more. Entering a
room looking for something, you do not stand and say:
"Here or There or There." You look about and move
slowly about, pausing, taking second views, etc.
(Actually, it all depends. But in any case with respect to
Socrates' subjects, one must grope—step forward and
perhaps back again and shuffling along, turning and
feeling one's way—slowly—perhaps like my working at
hedonism.)

W. reads Plato—the only philosopher he reads. But
he likes best the allegories, the myths. They're fine. He
made fun of these stool pigeons in the dialogues. He cited
the *Parmenides* as a dialogue in which although you got
no discussion you also got no pretense of any discussion.
In contrast is the *Theaetetus*. The young man Theaetetus
is introduced as a promising, bright youngster, but he
shows none of this. He has no fight in him at all. Why
doesn't he make a stand? Socrates arguing with these
weaklings!

By this time we had begun walking back. I asked
him again: You said that you did not understand—and
they didn't either—such sentences as: God is a spirit. I
meant to go on, but he took me up. I had apparently
misunderstood him. To understand such a sentence one
must note the context in which it is used. It is perhaps
introduced among idolators—worshippers of sticks and
stones. (Are there such worshippers?) To them this says:
God is not sticks and stones, God has no body. So far
then we understand this; but there is more. God is
prayed to, he is like a person. He hears and answers
prayer.

We walked along for some way and he came back

to the subject. There is an independent use of the phrase "The Spirit of the Lord": What is the passage in Luke where Jesus reads from Isaiah? (I was stupid as usual). "The spirit of the Lord is on me. (I looked it up last night after we returned from the Bucks' where we had dinner.) Here, of course, the use of the phrase is the same as the Inspirer. What Inspires?

I imagine that the religious, the fervent in prayer, etc., understand these phrases.

It amazes me how eager and how grasping and tightly grasping he must be when he reads. How lazy I always am. In all the years of going to church how lazily I've listened. But he, when he reads, what he reads is in bright gold and shining and it is for so long imprinted and ready in his mind.

September 16

YESTERDAY I WALKED OUT about five o'clock—it had rained hard earlier—to meet W. and to avoid his having to walk up our stairs. Again we walked towards the meadows. He began talking about his having seen a snake the day before, the first snake he had seen in England. Someone had told him that it was not poisonous, a garden snake, a yard long. He was surprised that snakes were common in the wilds in the United States, that I had once killed a rattlesnake, that many snakes are killed on the highways. We talked about the age of the very large trees there. His estimate was two hundred, three hundred years. As old as the colleges, perhaps. A forester could tell. Counted rings. Later he showed me how the Cherwell and Isis and Thames flow. The college boats were moored alongside and he noticed the emblems. One was the three lions which I think is All Souls.

Then I brought up this question: When you say, Men do desire pleasure, what is this use of "pleasure?" Is it contrasted with pain? Pain is localized, for instance.

He went on with one of the nicest bits of analysis I have heard, like some of those last summer on determinism, freedom, etc. He was, as he said, translating from what he has written, his book, no doubt. He started: Pain is a sensation. Pleasure is not. Then he went on to discuss the use of the word sensation—senses, etc., in psychology—as psychological concepts. Why are the senses—sight, hearing, smelling, taste, touch—classified together? Obviously, they are not a bit alike. Smells, odors, aren't a bit like sounds. Then he gave this account. With respect to all these, you can time them precisely with a clock. "Now you see; now you don't. Now you hear it; now you don't." And so with smelling, tasting, feeling (pressure, for instance). By the clock you can tell. This is not at all how it is with grief. It makes no sense to say that at 2 o'clock sharp I began to grieve, and at 2:15 I stopped. This then shows how sensations are distinguished from emotions.

Now pain is also like these sensations. It is a sensation in the same way in which sounds, sights, etc., are. Now you feel the pain; now you don't. When did it begin; when did it cease? Now pleasure isn't like this. The logic of the word "pleasure" is quite different. Clock the pleasure. When did the pleasure begin, when did the pleasure end, etc.? Does this make sense? Pain is also unlike sound sensations in a certain respect. Pain is in the head or in the shins. Where is the smell, the sound, the sight? Pressures are more like pains, and so are tastes. Where does it pinch or brush your cheek? Where are tastes? In the mouth. Sounds are not heard in the ear, nor are sights seen in the eye. So pain is a sensation. I am not clear as yet that there is no use of the word "pleasure," such that pleasure is not a sensation. I suppose that what I am confusing is pleasure and pleasant tastes, pleasant touches (tickles, caresses). This is terribly important. A tickle and a taste may at one time be pleasant and at another not pleasant. This brings out the difference.

There is however also a good reason why pain, although a sensation, should be classified with pleasure, which is no sensation. The reason is that both pain and pleasure are registered in the face, the eyes, the posture. Is he in pain? Look at him. Is he having a good time? Look at him.

It is in W.'s seeing such things as these—these similarities and these differences that the marvel of W.'s mind is so evident. Certainly I've known no one like him.

W. also said: There are no kinesthetic sensations. Of course you know with your eyes closed that you are now standing, but there are no sensations. And there may be organs in your joints such that if you did not have them you would not know that you were crooking your finger. But there are no sensations. Rubbish! Rubbish!

And James is wrong about emotions.

Earlier he also spoke of Moore again. He had seen Moore lately. Moore is good. Moore thinks hard. W. is going to Cambridge, next week, to see the doctor. How did he happen to speak of Moore?

Nearer home we peeked into Merton, one of the oldest colleges. "Old buildings!"

"What is the origin of the expression: 'fox trot'?
The dictionary of American slang—now that is a book
I could enjoy." I said I'd get him one.

He asked about Willis Doney and about John
Nelson. Nelson struck him as a very intelligent fellow.
And Gregory Vlastos was nice. Americans' individuality
he liked. But the politicians! Truman. His talk to the
journalists!

"The English say the elm is a treacherous tree.
The limbs fall off, break, not during the storm when you
would expect it, but afterward. And then it might hit
you."

W. stayed for dinner. The liveliness of his wit, his
imagination, is amazing. He talked about Shakespeare
at Stratford, the theatre, about Gretchen's new uniform,
about the woman who wished her children to express
their personalities, about his aunt who recommended a
recipe to his mother, and then later from her home sent
two samples, one as the cakes ought to be and one as
they ought not to be, about Dr. Louise Mooney again, his
doctor in Ithaca. After dinner, in the living room he told
me about Rush Rhees. About some performance of Lear
put on by the students at Cambridge—the best Shakespeare he ever saw.

September 25

Yesterday, Sunday afternoon, W. came up again. He
is amazingly kind and friendly to us. I don't understand
it. He is so severe in his judgment generally and yet he
seems so gentle with me. He sat down first for a little in
the living room. Gretchen and Eleanor both had very bad

colds. Then we took our walk in the meadows again. Our
talk was desultory since I proposed nothing. We talked
about many things. As we passed Merton Tower he
remarked that he liked it as one of the finest about in the
style of English Gothic. I began telling him about the
redwood trees—five thousand years old—very hard—
invulnerable to disease, but some dead at the top from
lightning. He knew about their great size.

As we walked along he threw nuts to a chaffinch
but the poor bird—very beautiful—was too shy. Just
nearby on the other side was a woman with a squirrel in
her arm. No dogs—so squirrels. He had earlier told us
about a tit which perched in his hand—flew to a tree, and
later as he approached it again, it perched on his uplifted
hand. He now described it to me and pointed out the
trees from which it had alighted upon his hand. English
robins are tame too. He had never seen a cardinal. Did
they have strong and broad beaks for eating grain or
longer and pointed ones for feeding on insects? Do they?

I asked him about Miss Elizabeth Anscombe, and
about Smythies. At some length again he told me about
them. Smythies never saying a word—for three years
until some Canadian-Edinburgh student by the name of
Taylor brought them together. Taylor who later was
killed in a brawl in Sydney, I think, on his way to a job in
Melbourne. He too W. tried to dissuade from philosophy.
A manly, energetic and tense person he was—very
industrious—full of tension—another more active life
would have suited him better. Though Miss Anscombe
is in Oxford she does not see much of Oxford philosophers. She goes to meetings of the Socratic Club—a
mistake, perhaps—and to the Jowett Club. Returning,
we saw a swan in the Cherwell. Swans preparing for

flight are a spectacle. They make a great whoosh and
noise with their great strong wings. A swan can break
a man's arm with his wings. And in flight, his neck
stretches straight and his feet outstretched behind is a
sight. Swans live in families—not in great flocks like
ducks and geese. He fed a squirrel clinging to a tree and
coaxed it into his arm. He was curious whether it was
the same squirrel we had seen earlier on the other side.
He thought not. He talked about the passing of the
brown squirrel (I think) in Europe. Then our brown and
gray squirrels.

As we passed along Merton he admired a small
reddish-leaved tree, and he noticed again the tower of
Merton, and the age of the chapel. The superstructure
was built later. One can see it. "Stern, isn't it?"—the
tower.

At supper he ate applesauce. Later he talked about
coconuts—the taste. He does not like any of the melon
family—squashes, melons, cucumbers. Before he left
he arranged for Miss Anscombe to come to tea today.

And this afternoon she came. She is stocky,
came in slacks and a man's jacket. She holds a research
fellowship—350 pounds. What a trifle! But does almost
no tutoring. Next term she will lecture....

W. talks about men as serious and deep. Perhaps
it's just that these men [philosophers referred to by Miss
Anscombe in the deleted section above] strike Miss
Anscombe as like magicians who with a certain trickery
and sleight of hand expose the poor ninny philosophers
whom they seize upon. The ninny philosophers may not
have had the benefit of borrowed cleverness, but they
were very earnest, they had problems to which they gave
their lives and hard labor. These people have nothing to

do but debunk. They are the hollow men sounding. It is not then that these people are mistaken in what they say. It is that they have nothing but this show they put on. What a clever boy I am! W. talked too about his own work. "It's not important but if anyone is interested I'm good at it and I may help. I don't recommend it. It's for people who cannot leave it alone." So this is not important. What is important must fall outside. And suppose there is nothing outside! Poor souls! Very well, these other philosophers made mistakes, in earnest, but what now are you doing in earnest? There you are crowing over the mistakes of earnest men. So you will never make an important mistake, for nothing is important to you. Wonderful! Crow!

October 2

HERE ARE a few sentences from W.:
> The sense of the world must lie outside the world. In it there is no value, it must lie outside all happening and being-so. It must lie outside the world.
>
> Ethics and aesthetics are one.
>
> The world of the happy is quite another than that of the unhappy.
>
> The solution of the riddle of life in space and time lies outside space and time.

November 28

THIS AFTERNOON WHEN I RETURNED HOME from bringing the rent to Brooks', W. was at my door below. Having found no one at home he was leaving, but returned again upstairs with me, apologetic about his looks. He hadn't shaved. This was his first visit since September. He had been to Norway. His vacation there was not too successful since his friend, Ben, was sick. But the weather was fine there.

We talked about Miss Anscombe to whom we had been "enormously kind." She is in the hospital and we had brought her some fruit. And about Smythies. He talked a little about Norway. Had I done any reading? Yes. *Notes from Underground.* Smythies had directed me to it. W. had read them a few years ago but he did not know what to make of them. He was puzzled that a man who could so clearly see and understand his own humiliation should not change. One could imagine a man who acted as he did but who never reflected, should continue in the same old rut. But not him. Such a man would at least come to adjust himself, even by some sort of technique, to avoid such misuses.

We got around to discussing Smythies' suggestion that the author of the *Notes* was trying to give himself a character. W. could understand that. That would be like trying to give oneself a style. And so there might be such a thing as a style of living. A young English boy goes to the local school and then to Eton. He cultivates a style of living. He is trained to become angry on certain occasions, to blame on certain occasions, etc. This was not much to the point though it was a nice explanation of giving oneself a style. Usually someone else gives one a style. We finally did get around to distinguishing between the two parts of the *Notes* and talking then about the first.

intelligently, with such discernment of what he reads.
This man taught with W. in Austria.

(In listening to W. talk about his friend I realized
how he dramatizes these recollections of his. Oh, how
his friend could talk about a book he had read!)

Someone had once asked him to help in translating Rilke. Translating lyric poetry! Of course, he
wouldn't. That prose book of Rilke's [*The Notebooks
of Malte Laurids Brigge*] he had read too. Too precious!
Not good for Gretchen. History of the past, settled
history would be better. Her going to lectures on Shakespeare would be bad. She would then read Shakespeare to
find what the lecturer found. He himself can still make
nothing of Shakespeare. And now Gretchen will. Well,
maybe. I wonder how he talks about Shakespeare.

January 11, 1951

YESTERDAY AFTERNOON I WENT to see W. to carry him the
bottle of Christmas port, and a jar of applesauce. Miss
Anscombe had called the day before to tell us that he was
sick. He has quite severe pains that begin in the morning
and cease about four in the afternoon. He was in bed and
looked amazingly sweet and mild. He invited me to sit
down and stay and when I thought I should leave he
urged me to stay longer. The doctor does not know or
will not say what ails him.

Speaking of Smythies he said that he stands out as
in a field of grain, not the common sort. What a figure!
And how like W. himself.

He did ask me about events in Korea, and how old
MacArthur was.

He is almost fanatical about cleanliness. Even
now when he is ill, he gets up for his bath every morning.
He's supposed to lie quiet. And this is not a perfunctory
matter. He scrubs vigorously. And it takes him an hour.
At Cambridge he used to heat buckets and buckets of
water for his bath in his room.

Miss Anscombe said that during the war he once
returned the money Cambridge paid him for lectures:
"The lectures were no good, not worth the money."
They were, of course, better than any others given.

This evening I saw Chadbourne Gilpatrick
[director of the Rockefeller Foundation] in the Mitre.
He'd been to see W. this afternoon to offer him money.
W. was quite agreeable, and apparently agreed to let them
know if he should again be in condition to work. When
Gilpatrick suggested that money be used to print any
papers that he might have—the world needed them
badly—W. said: "But see, I write one sentence, and then
I write another—just the opposite. And which shall
stand?"

Again he said something about the rot people
publish, going on writing after they've stopped thinking. They don't know when to quit. Russell!

January 16

ON SATURDAY I SAW W. He was in pain, and had been since
morning. He was obviously quite despondent. At one
point he said: "I'd not mind now if ..." and then he
turned to me and said he wouldn't finish the sentence.
He said he would write to his doctor in Cambridge about

seeing a specialist. But he would not go to an English
hospital. He would rather die here in his own room.
Today he should have a letter from Cambridge.

Nevertheless he talked and wanted me to stay. He
told me again about his doctor in Ithaca. It did not occur
to him that he had told me about that twice before. Then
he told me about his visit to New York in 1939. The
people were awful. Only one person he liked, an Italian
boy in Central Park who shined his shoes twice. The boy
hoped someday to shine shoes in a better location. He
was genuine. W. paid double for his shine.

He stayed in a large hotel on Lexington Avenue
off from—opposite—Rockefeller Center on Fifth Avenue. He couldn't sleep for noise, even on the twenty-
seventh story.

On the last day just before he left he took a taxi to
see a doctor in New Jersey. Going through the tunnel the
taxi driver shut off the fare meter. It stood at four dollars
and W. saw it. The taxi driver stopped just beyond the
tunnel and told W. the fare was seven dollars. W. got out,
undecided. Then he went up to a policeman standing
by and told him what had happened. Should he pay?
The policeman went up, seized the driver by the neck,
wrenched him out of the cab, and said to W.: Pay
him $4.50.

He was glad to get on a boat—Holland-American
line—away from America....

Later he managed to sit on the edge of the bed and
felt some better.

On Sunday Gretchen and I went to see him. She
brought four eggs. He was not in such pain, but I think he

was weaker. He grew tired as he tried to pay us some attention.

He talked about thunderstorms. One of his sisters was very fond of them, and they were terrific in the Alps where his father had a summer home. Another sister was frightened of them and used to hide. She was cured once when she and a friend were walking through a forest in the mountains, and were overtaken by a storm. After that she did not mind.

Yesterday Miss Anscombe said that he was growing weaker. No wonder. On Sunday he said he was not going to eat any more porridge. He eats almost nothing at all. No one says a word about cancer.

On Saturday in the very act of turning to avoid a pain he asked if I had ever heard of Couéism. I had: "Every day in every way I am feeling better and better." He remembered the sentence. I said I thought it might help if you could believe it. He said: Yes, since fear is a part of one's ailment, saying this might help to allay fear. His mind was still as clear as could be.

He said Gilpatrick had been to see him. At first Gilpatrick began talking about language and philosophy—the patter. W. cut that off short. And then he talked sense. W. told him that if, as was unlikely, he would be able to write again, he would write to him. But W. told me that he did not think that he would ever have a discussion with me again. He had hoped that he and Smythies and I might have a discussion together sometime.

On Sunday, he also talked about his down comforter.

FURTHER READING

By Wittgenstein

Tractatus Logico-Philosophicus. New translation, D. F. Pears and B. F. McGuiness. London: Routledge & Kegan Paul, 1961.

The Blue and Brown Books, ed. Rush Rhees. Oxford: Basil Blackwell, 1958.

Philosophical Investigations, ed. G. E. M. Anscombe and Rush Rhees, trans. G. E. M. Anscombe. Oxford: Basil Blackwell, 1953; 2d ed., 1958.

Zettel, ed. G. E. M. Anscombe and G. H. von Wright, trans. G. E. M. Anscombe. Oxford: Basil Blackwell, 1967.

On Certainty, ed. G. E. M. Anscombe and G. H. von Wright; trans. G. E. M. Anscombe and Denis Paul. Oxford: Basil Blackwell, 1969.

Culture and Value, ed. G. H. von Wright, trans. Peter Winch. Chicago: University of Chicago Press, 1980.